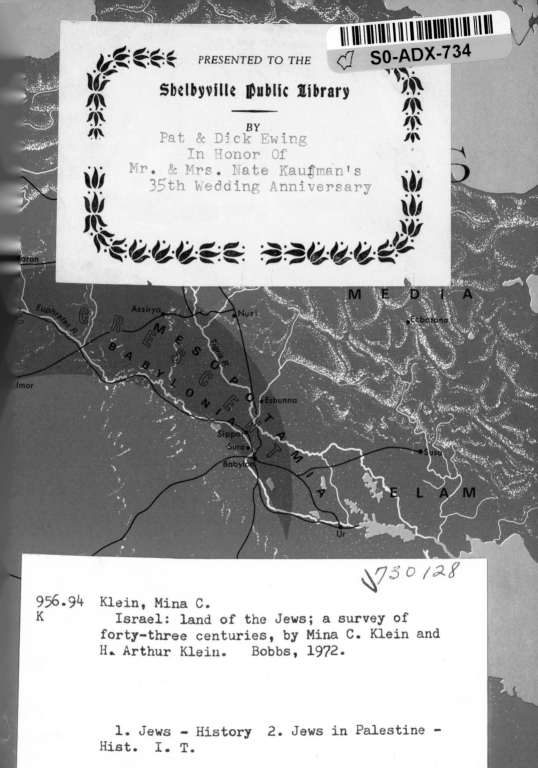

PRESENTED TO THE

Shelbyville Public Library

BY
Pat & Dick Ewing
In Honor Of
Mr. & Mrs. Nate Kaufman's
35th Wedding Anniversary

S0-ADX-734

√730128

956.94   Klein, Mina C.
K   Israel: land of the Jews; a survey of
        forty-three centuries, by Mina C. Klein and
        H. Arthur Klein.   Bobbs, 1972.

            1. Jews - History 2. Jews in Palestine -
        Hist. I. T.

ISRAEL

LAND OF THE JEWS

A Survey of Forty-Three Centuries

ISR

AEL

LAND OF
THE JEWS

A SURVEY OF FORTY-THREE CENTURIES

BY MINA C. KLEIN
AND H. ARTHUR KLEIN

THE BOBBS-MERRILL COMPANY, INC.
INDIANAPOLIS NEW YORK

078735

THE BOBBS-MERRILL COMPANY, INC.

A SUBSIDIARY OF HOWARD W. SAMS & CO., INC.

PUBLISHERS   INDIANAPOLIS   KANSAS CITY   NEW YORK

Copyright © 1972 by H. Arthur Klein and Mina C. Klein

Members of the Authors League of America

Maps by Carta of Jerusalem

Design by Jack Jaget

Printed in the United States of America

All rights reserved

Library of Congress catalog card number: 71-156115

0 9 8 7 6 5 4 3 2 1

To
MICHAEL AVI-YONAH
of Jerusalem, Israel,
generous and gifted
preserver of a great past

730128

ACKNOWLEDGMENTS

The authors are primarily indebted for encouragement, counsel, and correction to the distinguished scholar, Dr. Michael Avi-Yonah.

Thanks are extended also to two library systems whose facilities assisted in the research for the history here presented:

The Los Angeles County Library—and especially to Mrs. Evelyne Hamilton, librarian of its Malibu branch, and Mrs. Deborah B. Wilds, regional librarian, as well as to their staffs.

The UCLA Library—via Dr. Robert Vosper, university librarian, and many helpful members of his staff.

The authors venture also to reiterate the obvious: they are wholly and solely responsible for such errors of fact or interpretation as may persist despite all efforts to eliminate them.

CONTENTS

CONTENTS

A PREFATORY NOTE ON NAMES, BOUNDARIES, AND BACKGROUND

The history of Israel is varied and violence-studded; its peoples have been beset by conquests, rebellions, internal strife, enslavements, and forced exiles. Inevitably, the regions of residence and rule have shifted, and the names given to them have changed. Israel therefore has been variously known as Canaan, as the realms of David and Solomon, as the separate kingdoms of Judah and Israel, as Yehud, Judea, Palestine, the Holy Land, and *Eretz Yisrael*—the land of Israel.

Encompassing all the diverse place-names, however, is the larger concept of the Jewish homeland, that part of the world within which all the "lands" referred to in this history have been located.

In its largest outlines that land lies between the Mediterranean in the west and the desert in the east; between the sources of the Jordan River in the north and Sinai in the south. The Jordan is its principal river, the lake of Galilee and the Dead Sea its principal bodies of water.

Jerusalem became and has remained, in an undeniable sense, the jewel and ornament of this land. There have been important periods when Jerusalem was not the center of government or administration, but from the time of its establishment as David's capital in about 1000 B.C.E. it has never ceased to be the Jewish people's center of gravity and of aspiration.

So knowledgeable an historian as the Reverend James Parkes, author of *History of Palestine* (1949) and of the more recent *Whose Land?* concludes that through the centuries the region

[11]

called Palestine became a national home for the Jews, and for no other definable people. The following pages present the highlights in the striking and sometimes improbable story of how this small strip of land became so indelibly associated with the Jewish people.

1

THE "PROMISED LAND" THAT ABRAM ENTERED

(TO ABOUT 1500 B.C.E.)

You, O Lord, are the God who chose Abram,
who brought him out of Ur of the Chaldees
and named him Abra-ham.
—NEHEMIAH 9:7

Size alone does not make a place important in history. The most striking example of this is a small area of land known by many famous names—Canaan, Palestine, Judea, the Holy Land, and *Eretz Yisrael*, which translated from the Hebrew means the Land of Israel. The people who were forced to leave it dreamed, planned, and struggled somehow to return, if only as pilgrims, or to spend there the last years of their lives, or even just to be buried in its soil.

No other one name among the many that have been given to this little land during the past three or four thousand years is so meaningful as *Israel—Land of the Jews*. Looking down from a modern jet plane or examining a map in an atlas, one may well wonder how it came to loom so large in men's minds. It is minor in size; it is largely arid and otherwise ill favored by nature.

In past millennia the Mediterranean, then called "the Great Sea," was the center around which the important peoples and nations of the world were clustered.

East of the modern nations of Israel and Jordan lie the desert regions of the enormous Arabian peninsula. In the days before petroleum became a power in the world, the deserts meant to men mostly obstacles to be endured or overcome, and those regions bred tough and resourceful peoples, bold or rash in attitude and action, and notably unwilling to endure oppression without resisting it.

The great deserts of central Arabia were rimmed on the north by overarching areas of land that was fertile because it was relatively well watered. The shape of these regions of green growing things has led geographers and historians to call them "the Fertile Crescent."

At the southwestern tip or horn of this imaginary crescent lies Israel itself. At the opposite or southeastern end two famous rivers, the Tigris and the Euphrates, flow into the Persian Gulf. The arable plains between these rivers were named *Mesopotamia* —"between-river-land"—by the Greeks.

The part of the earth that came to be called Israel is bounded largely by water on the west, by wilderness wastes and water to the south, by the great deserts to the east, and by mountainous regions to the north. Its limits have never been sharply defined and its terrain is varied and contrasting. In its southern part lies the *Negev*, the great wilderness that extends all the way to the north-ernmost arm of the Red Sea—the Gulf of Eilat, also known today as the Gulf of Aqaba or Akaba. Eilat, spelled sometimes Elat or Elath, is a well-known city in modern Israel, while less than ten miles east of it lies Aqaba, a town in modern Jordan.

West of the Gulf of Eilat lies the great triangle of the Sinai peninsula, and still farther west the Gulf of Suez, while beyond that is the mighty continent of Africa itself.

Through Israel from north to south flows the remarkable Jordan River. It passes first through the small but historic Sea of Galilee, which is known also by such names as Lake Chin-nereth, Lake Gennezareth, and Lake Tiberias. South of that sea the Jordan winds ever deeper into a great natural cleft of the earth, finally reaching the Dead Sea, whose surface lies 1,300 feet below the level of the nearby Mediterranean.

Thus tiny Israel forms both the southernmost corner of the Fertile Crescent, and a link between that crescent and the other great fertile region of antiquity, the valley of the Nile River. The central arch or thickest part of the Fertile Crescent includes important portions of the nations now called Lebanon, Syria (southern and western parts), Turkey (southern part), and Iraq (which includes much of the important ancient region of Meso-potamia).

We in modern times are prone to think that the most important parts of the world lie west and northwest of Israel: Europe, the United States, and other so-called western nations. However, to the earliest inhabitants of that region it was the east that was most important. A man facing the rising sun in the east would find the north on his left and the south on his right. Thus in the ancient Hebrew language the word that meant *forward* or *ahead* was also the word that meant *eastward*. Similarly, the word for *right* (hand) meant also *south*, and that for *left* meant *north*. Among the Hebrew tribes who came to live in what later became the Kingdom of Israel, the most southerly district was held by *Benjamin*, whose name meant "son of the south." If there were early Hebrew charts, they surely would have been drawn with the east on top, in the dominant position, just as our maps are drawn with the north on top.

This eastward emphasis arose because of the eastern origins of the residents of the land that came to be Israel. They were descended from wave after wave of nomads who had emerged from the harsh desert regions to the east and had infiltrated or fought their way into the far more attractive and promising lands closer to the Mediterranean.

Traveling down from the northeast through what is now coastal Lebanon and southern Syria, Bedouin-like groups, families, or entire clans came down into Israel with their herds and flocks. They too entered the land that was to become sacred to the three great religions of the western world.

What are now Israel and Jordan had not been unpopulated before these great migrations from the outside. There were primitive settlements and communities at a number of sites. At Jericho, for example, human remains dating back about nine thousand years have been found. Significant ancient relics have been discovered elsewhere also. However, the enormous historical importance of the land of Israel derives from the men and women who moved into it rather than from those who lived there in prehistoric times.

The unique and strategic location of the land we now call Israel made it a target or at least a way point in major early movements of tribes and in later years of merchants and men of affairs traveling to and from the east. In short, Israel was the natural

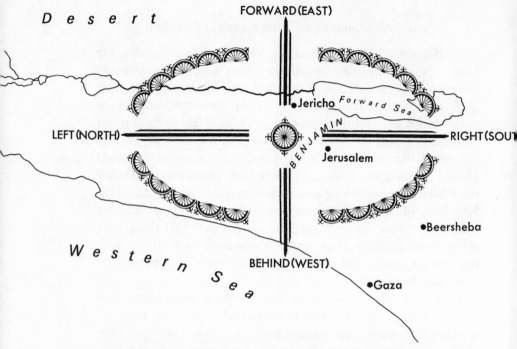

Early Hebrew charts would have been drawn with the East on top.

link between Mesopotamia with the rich valleys of the Tigris-Euphrates river systems on the one hand, and the great fertile, inviting valley of the Nile River, from which Egypt arose, on the other.

In these two latter regions men first developed large-scale organized agriculture based on irrigation—the planned, cooperative, and continuing use of water supplies. It was in Mesopotamia first, and the Nile Valley not long afterward, that the social results of this new type of production showed themselves: in Mesopotamia arose the world's first great examples of city culture; in Egypt, somewhat later, developed the first great centralized powers, whose territory included many cities and towns.

These regimes commanded considerable expanses of territory, united for rule, for exploitation, for taxation, for defense, and even for external conquest. Such regimes, whether concentrated around one central ruling city, or including a number of cities and towns, are commonly called "civilizations"—even when they engage in very "uncivilized" behavior.

[18]

In Mesopotamia there appeared a whole series of such city-state organizations, identified usually by the names of the population centers in which their rulers and tax-collectors resided: Akkad, Ur (which ruled over Sumer), Babylon, and others. Even three or four thousand years before the Christian era (B.C.E.), the great "civilized" regimes of the Mesopotamian plains were not cut off completely from the Nile region (Egypt). The main road connecting the two became a busy highway for caravans and foot travelers. And it led through the very region we now call Israel.

In fact, this land-link eventually contained not one but two great roads. One, along the coast, was called the *Via Maris;* the other, farther inland, east of the Jordan valley, was known as the King's Highway. The latter road ran all the way from the important center of Damascus in the north to Eilat at the head of the Gulf of Aqaba in the south. From Eilat the route ran westward past the head of the Gulf of Suez, to the Nileside center near where the great city of Cairo now stands.

Thus the territory that became Israel was crossed by the only major trails along which travelers, traders, settlers, soldiers, slaves, priests, prophets, or princes moved between Mesopotamia and Egypt. By the time sailors became bold or skillful enough to take their small craft far into the Mediterranean, Israel's "crossroads of the world" site had already made it a natural meeting place as well as a mixing or melting pot for the most dynamic and influential societies of the very ancient world.

The oldest known records of names or events in this land of Israel are found in one of the two major regions that it links. At Abydos, Egypt, was discovered an inscription in honor of an army commander who had served a pharaoh with the lively name of Pepi the First. It tells of a military campaign around 2350 B.C.E. into the land of the Sand-Dwellers, as the Egyptians then called the inhabitants of the region which now includes the great port city of Haifa somewhat south of Lebanon. A little north of that Haifa site the Egyptian marines had made an amphibious landing, while their foot soldiers slogged northward along the coast. Together they attacked fortifications, raided settlements, destroyed orchards and vineyards, and—like so many of the armies that have invaded Israel during the twenty-three centuries since—made off with much booty.

Not long before 2000 B.C.E. the first important wave of nomadic in-wanderers arrived in Israel from the western edges of the great Arabian desert. These peoples were properly called the *Amorites*, and they resided in the region just east of the Dead Sea. A little farther north, but still east of the Jordan, were the *Ammonite* people. (The name Amorite is used several times in the Bible also to refer to some west-of-Jordan inhabitants of Canaan.) Modern archeologists have discovered relics proving that the east-of-Jordan Amorites had attained impressive skills in shaping pottery and in making tools or weapons from copper—then the most advanced metal for man, since the Age of Iron had not yet dawned.

By roughly 2000 B.C.E., descendants of these nomadic invaders inhabited the principal towns of Israel and had almost surely interbred with the remaining earlier inhabitants. By about 1950 B.C.E. this new population was causing trouble for the rulers of Egypt—a situation that was to be repeated often in later ages. In the Egyptian cities of Sakkara and Thebes have been found ancient clay figures inscribed with curses against rebellious and anti-Egyptian rulers of towns in the land that became Israel. These indignant records are called "the execration texts." One group mentions a town at the site of what later became the pivotal city of Jerusalem. Another group, dating to about 1850 B.C.E., lists by name more than sixty different towns, each with only one ruler or local king. It seems certain that in these towns the once-nomadic Amorites had settled down to stable living.

At just about this time, approximately in the eighteenth century B.C.E., must be placed the events or changes that are summarized or symbolized in the Bible's first book, *Genesis*, by the fabulous figure of Abram or Abraham. His story in Genesis relates, in a single narrative, events that must have occurred over many centu-

ries. Abram, it tells, came from the city of Ur of the Chaldees. Ur
lay, in fact, on the Euphrates about 175 miles southeast of Babylon, but the Chaldeans did not hold sway there until 500 years or
more after Abram's presumed lifetime. During the actual time of
Abram, Ur was a center of the older Sumerian culture, which
reached its peak about 2000 B.C.E.

According to the story, Abram moved from Ur northwestward, following the Euphrates toward its sources, passing the
sites of Babylon and Mari. For a time he and his retinue settled at
Haran near the peak or crest of the Fertile Crescent and within
what is now Turkey. It was then a city in the land of the Ara-
means known as Padan-Aram. Genesis tells us that *Terah* was
Abram's father, *Nahor* his grandfather, and *Serug* his great-grand-
father. All of these are actually names of places or villages near
Haran. Apparently the ancestors of Abram lived long in this
region, which lies some 120 miles east and south of the present
city of Aleppo, Syria, and not far from where the borders of modern Turkey and Iraq meet.

Genesis tells how God instructed Abram to leave this region, to
forsake his relatives and the house of his father, and to move on
south into a land that would be revealed to him and given to him
and his descendants. That command was accompanied by a promise, or "covenant": Abram's descendants would become a great
and numerous people, and his name would come to be so great that
it would serve to bless those who blessed him and curse those who
cursed him. Finally—and most meaningful to us in these troubled
modern days—God promised that Abram would become a means
of reconciliation and peace among the peoples of the earth.

Already seventy-five years old, Abram did as he was told. He
set out southward. With him was his childless wife, Sarai, his
nephew Lot, and all their possessions, mostly livestock, clothing,
and precious metals. Their route took them through Aleppo,
Qatna, and Damascus. They paused at Shechem, near Mount
Gerizim and about 45 miles north of a place then called Salem,
now famous as Jerusalem. This Shechem, near the town today
called Nablus, was even then a sacred place, or sanctuary, for the

[21]

inhabitants of the land. Here stood a tree of oracles or prophecy —a *terebinth*, of the sumac family. And here God appeared to Abram, promising to give "this land to your descendants."

Abram built an altar at Shechem, then again moved southward to the hills east of Beth-el, about twelve miles north of modern Jerusalem. There he erected another altar to the God who had singled him out. Southward he moved again, through Beersheba and into the great Negev, today an arid region. Even then a famine had the land in its grip, so Abram went on farther south and then west into Egypt itself.

Writers in the later "Kingdom of Judah" (part of what is now Israel) inserted into the Abram narrative a strange episode in Egypt. Just before they entered that land of the Nile, Abram told his wife, Sarai, that her great beauty might tempt the Egyptians to kill him in order to keep her. Hence he asked her to pose as his sister, "so that for your sake I may be well treated and my life be spared."

Sarai's beauty did indeed excite the courtiers of the pharaoh. They praised her highly, and she was taken into the king's household and harem. The pharaoh treated her "brother" Abram well, presenting him with sheep, cattle, camels, asses, and human slaves, both male and female. However, serious illness struck the pharaoh and his household, for God was displeased by the deception. Discovering the true situation, the pharaoh protested to Abram, "What have you done to me? Why did you not tell me she was your wife? . . . Take your wife, and leave at once!"

With his many belongings Abram returned to the land (Israel) that God had promised him. By now the herds of Abram and Lot were so numerous that the land could not support them all together. Hence Abram proposed that they go separate ways. Lot moved east into the Jordan plain; Abram remained farther west, in the part of Israel that in Genesis is called the land of Canaan. Again God spoke, telling Abram to look about in every direction: "All the land you see I will give to you and your descendants forever. I will make your descendants as numerous as the dust of the earth." He told Abram also to "walk about in the land, through its length and breadth, for to you will I give it."

The remainder of the Abram story in Genesis is complex and sometimes contradictory. Abram fathered a son, Ishmael, by Hagar, the maidservant of Sarai. Then, when he was one hundred years old and Sarai ninety-nine, God again appeared and revealed that they were at last to have a son of their own. In spite of Abram's disbelief, Isaac was born to them.

Now known by their somewhat altered names of Abra-ham and Sara, they both lived to advanced ages. According to Genesis, Sara died at age 127, and Abraham at 175, after a very full life. Abraham's sons Ishmael and Isaac buried him in a cave on his own land in Hebron. The name Abra-ham has the very significant Hebrew meaning of "Father of the People."

2

HEBREWS
AS SLAVES IN EGYPT,
CONQUERORS
IN CANAAN,
AND FOES OF THE
PHILISTINES

(TO ABOUT 1025 B.C.E.)

You saw the afflictions of our fathers in Egypt,
     you heard their cry by the Red Sea . . .
The sea you divided before them,
     on dry ground they passed through . . .
Their pursuers you hurled into the depths . . .

With a column of cloud you led them by day,
     and by night with a column of fire . . .
On Mount Sinai you came down,
     you spoke with them from heaven;
You gave them just ordinances, firm laws,
     good statutes, and commandments . . .
     by the hand of Moses, your servant.

—NEHEMIAH 9:9-14

The relationships between the Bible and verifiable history are complex and fascinating. The Bible is rich in symbolism, allegory, legend, and folktales. Its chronicles, vivid and dramatic, were in fact written, revised, and rewritten many generations or even centuries later than the events which they describe. Most of the prophecies woven into the books of the Bible also were put into words long after the periods to which they apply.

Yet the Bible narratives are necessary for an understanding of what the land of Israel came to mean to the Jews who were its residents and defenders, and also to the enormous numbers of Jews who, by choice or necessity, lived out their lives far from the boundaries of little Israel itself.

Chapters 25–27 of Genesis deal with the life of Isaac; chapters 28–33 tell of the great journey made by Isaac's son Jacob. From Beersheba at the northern edge of the Negev, he returned all the way north to the place from which his grandfather Abraham had come—Haran, or Padan-Aram. There lived Jacob's uncle Laban, brother of Rebekah, the mother of Jacob and the wife of Isaac. Laban's two daughters, cousins to Jacob, were Leah the elder and Rachel the younger. Leah was nearsighted, but her sister Rachel was in all ways beautiful and well formed. In order to be allowed to wed Rachel, Jacob labored for seven years tending Laban's flocks. But after their marriage was consummated, he found that it was Leah who had been given to him as his bride. After still another seven years' hard labor for Laban he was allowed to marry Rachel also.

Jacob fathered a number of sons whose names are those of the principal tribes of the Hebrews who settled in the land we call Israel. Each name, by its meaning or sound, had its own particular interpretation or symbolic sense. Leah's first four sons were Reuben ("Behold, a son!"); Simeon ("hearing"); Levi ("attachment"); and Judah ("praise"). Rachel, disappointingly childless, gave to Jacob her maidservant Bilhah, who became the mother of Dan ("he brought vindication") and Naphtali ("trick"). Leah also gave to Jacob her own maid, Zilpah, who became the mother of Gad ("luck") and Asher ("fortune"). Leah herself later gave birth to a fifth son, Issachar ("reward"), and a sixth, Zebulun ("gift"). Then a seventh child was born to Leah, a daughter named Dinah. At last Rachel too bore a child of her own, Joseph ("may he add").

Finally, after some twenty years' hard service to Laban, Jacob, with his family, his many flocks and his servants, left Laban to return to his birthplace in the land the Lord had assigned to his grandfather Abraham. The homeward journey took Jacob past Ramoth-Gilead, to the ford across the Jabbok River. There he sent the rest of the company ahead, while he remained behind alone. That night there appeared to him a man, or what seemed to be a man, with whom he wrestled all night long. When daylight came Jacob's thigh had been dislocated, but still he would not release his grip on his adversary.

Finally the stranger begged, "Let me go!"

But Jacob answered in these haunting words, "I will not, unless first you bless me!"

"What are you called?" asked the stranger.

"Jacob."

"Then from now on your name shall not be Jacob, but Isra-el [meaning wrestler with the Lord], for you have wrestled with God and man, and have been victorious."

"Please tell me *your* name," Jacob said. But the stranger answered with the question: "Why should you wish to know it?" Then he blessed Jacob and said farewell.

To that place, Jacob gave the name Peniel, meaning "the face of God," for, he said, "I have seen God face to face, yet remain alive." At sunrise Israel-Jacob left the site, a place in Gilead, elsewhere in the Bible called also Penuel.

On their further way homeward, the Genesis story tells, Dinah, daughter of Jacob, was desired and mistreated by Shechem, son of Hamor, ruler of the region in which they were traveling. Headed by Simeon and Levi, Jacob's sons took a terrible vengeance, for they tricked, trapped, and slew every man in the city (also called Shechem) and carried off most of its valuable property.

This grisly tale probably had its beginnings in some ancient armed conflict between early invading Israelite tribesmen and the natives of the region of Shechem, who were called Hurrians. Other oft-told word-of-mouth tales similarly evolved, after many changes and mergings, into further dramatic and passionate episodes in the Bible chronicles of the Founding Fathers: Abraham, Isaac, and Israel-Jacob with his many sons and their followers.

Rachel, favorite wife of Israel-Jacob, died en route to Hebron, their destination; earlier, however, she had given birth to Benjamin, "the son of the right hand, or south." Now Israel-Jacob had twelve sons, eleven of whom bore the names of the leading tribal groups among the Hebrews who had come from the desert regions and won a foothold in Canaan-Israel. In alphabetical order those sons were: Asher, Benjamin, Dan, Gad, Issachar, Judah, Levi, Naphtali, Reuben, Simeon, and Zebulun.

Alone among Jacob's twelve sons, Joseph did not bear the name of a tribe. A special destiny was in store for him. Once Israel-Jacob's family were safely settled at Hebron, the sons tended their aging father's large herds of livestock, the principal form of wealth for wandering tribes. Joseph, only seventeen, was clearly his father's favorite. He watched his brothers at their work and reported to his father how well or how poorly they did their tasks. Their dislike and jealousy of Joseph reached a climax when Israel-Jacob made a many-colored cloak for Joseph but none for the older brothers.

They were all sent to pasture their father's flocks far to the north. When Joseph followed to watch and report on them, they plotted to kill him. Only Reuben restrained them from outright murder. He persuaded them instead to strip off Joseph's cloak and to throw him into an empty cistern.

When a caravan happened along, bearing gum, balsam, and resin to sell in Egypt, the brothers decided to sell Joseph as a slave to the Arabian (Ishmaelite) caravan masters. A group of merchants from Midian, far to the south on the eastern shores of the Gulf of Aqaba, finally took Joseph into Egypt, where they sold him as a slave to Potiphar, chief steward and leading courtier of the reigning pharaoh.

A series of dramatic events raised Joseph from servitude to the favor of the pharaoh, who finally made Joseph his chief administrator in charge of welfare and food supplies for all Egypt. Under his new Egyptianized name of Zaphnath-paaneah, Joseph was given as wife the daughter of a prominent Egyptian priest. With her he fathered two sons, Manasseh and Ephraim. Their names, like those of Joseph's eleven brothers, duplicate the names of other leading Hebrew tribes who had entered the land of Canaan-Israel.

Genesis links the name Manasseh with "forgetting," because Joseph's new fortunes made him forget his earlier sufferings; and Ephraim with "fruitful," for God had made Joseph fruitful even in his Egyptian slavery.

Fruitfulness and plenty amidst shortages indeed were identified with the rest of Joseph's life. He was able to foresee that a period of good harvests and prosperity would be followed by one of hunger and famine. In the good years he gathered into storehouses great quantities of grain. When the bad years came, Joseph rationed out these reserves. They saved the masses of Egyptians from starvation, and peoples from outside Egypt entered the land to beg a share from the precious stores. Israel-Jacob, also facing starvation in his own land, sent his ten remaining sons to Egypt to buy grain. They humbly begged the pharaoh's mighty governor for permission to make these purchases, not realizing that he was the brother they had sold into slavery. Joseph recognized them, however. After a time he revealed his true identity and forgave the wrong they had done to him.

The pharaoh instructed Joseph to invite his father, his brothers, and their households, numbering seventy in all, to take up residence in Egypt, where they would "live off the fat of the land," and all the best should be theirs. They accepted and settled themselves in the land of Goshen, somewhat west of the present Suez Canal, where their flocks prospered so that they became rich.

In one of the dramatic confrontations that seem to sum up much of ancient history, Joseph presents his old father, Israel-Jacob, to the pharaoh, who asks, "How long have you lived?"

"I have lived 130 years as a wayfarer," the patriarch answers. "The days of my life have been few and hard; and they do not compare with the years that my ancestors lived as wayfarers."

Beyond doubt it was as wayfarers, or nomadic herdsmen, that the people known as Hebrews or Jews entered Egypt itself. The deeply moving human drama of Joseph and his brothers was the explanation evolved at a much later time to account for a cherished tradition: namely, that some, at least, of the ancestors of the Hebrews who came into Canaan and conquered it had previously lived and labored under hard conditions in Egypt, and then had left or escaped.

Historians today hold two slightly different theories. One is that the "children of Israel" went into Egypt during its so-called Hyksos period. The other theory is that their entry took place at a later time, during the rule of a native Egyptian pharaoh named Amenhotep.

Hyksos was an Egyptian name meaning "rulers of [or from] foreign lands." It was applied to the multitudes of dynamic and warlike desert-bred nomads who forced their way into Egypt, having first passed through Syria and Canaan-Israel. The Hyksos were fierce and highly mobile, depending for their striking power on their mounted shock troops, and pioneering with that early forerunner of the modern armored car, the horse-drawn war chariot. Egypt had been weakened by struggles between rival native rulers of its southern and northern regions. Hence the Hyksos were able to establish control over northern Egypt from about 1720 to 1570 B.C.E., a sizable period of one and one-half centuries.

At its peak, Hyksos power extended south and west from the

Euphrates River, deep into Egypt. But their alien overlordship in Egypt was finally shaken off. Pharaoh Ahmose I, founder of Egypt's eighteenth dynasty, drove them out and destroyed the leading Hyksos center of Zoan near the northern end of the present Suez Canal. He drove their forces across the great barren land-bridge of the Sinai peninsula, and even, after a three-year siege, took the town of Sharuhen near Israel's southern coast.

According to the "Hyksos theory," the residence of Hebrew tribesmen in northern Egypt came to an end soon after this expulsion of the Hyksos rulers.

The other theory, seemingly somewhat more strongly supported, suggests that Hebrew tribes settled in northern Egypt in the period from about 1400 to 1350 B.C.E., during the reign of Pharaoh Amenhotep III or Amenhotep IV. The latter, known also as Ikhn-aton, was a remarkable religious radical and reformer who tried to substitute one-god worship (monotheism) for many-god idolatry (polytheism), which was practiced by the wealthy and powerful priests of Egypt. These priests opposed him bitterly and reasserted their control after his early death.

According to this theory, the exodus or escape of the Hebrews from Egypt took place during the reign of Rameses II, a later pharaoh, early in the thirteenth century B.C.E.

By either theory, the total period of residence and then of labor or slavery of the Hebrews in Egypt lasted at most not more than 150 years and perhaps much less. Also, the period of the Egyptian "bondage" of the children of Israel must be placed within the 500 years between about 1720 and 1220 B.C.E.

The Genesis story, with its clarion call for freedom ("Let my people go!"), indicates convincingly that the original entry of the Hebrews into Egypt was permitted, but that their departure was opposed, and that they finally escaped under conditions of difficulty and danger. Pharaoh Rameses II decreed the building of great treasure cities, including one named after himself, using forced or slave labor to get them completed quickly. The Hebrew settlers indeed may have been among the oppressed workers who sweated under Egyptian taskmasters, being forced to "make bricks without straw," a very difficult assignment.

The *Exodus* story in the Bible, like much of Genesis, is vivid, complex, and sometimes baffling. It is dominated by the powerful and sometimes mysterious figure of Moses, a prince reared at the Egyptian court but turned rebel and freedom fighter. It includes the flight of the Israelites, with a miraculous crossing of the "Red Sea," which was quite possibly the Sea of Reeds along the Mediterranean coast rather than the Red Sea south of today's city of Eilat. This is followed by a surprisingly long period of forty years of "wandering" in the deserts and wilderness, during which time a new generation of Israelites was born and attained maturity.

Within this long nomadic period is placed the revelation of the divine law (the Ten Commandments) from Mount Sinai, with Moses as intermediary between God and his chosen people. Then follows the entry into and penetration of the longed-for "promised land" of Canaan (Israel), which—because of Abraham, Isaac, Jacob, and Joseph—seems more like a homecoming than an assault on a new territory. In any case, the Hebrew tribes did not come into an empty or unclaimed area. The residents already there were largely people of similar ancestry, though by now differing in languages, customs, and worship. These Canaanites were idolatrous, as later monotheistic Jewish writers repeatedly stressed.

Different parts of the Bible suggest different lengths of time required for the Hebrew tribes to establish their foothold in Canaan. The main outlines seem clear. It could not have been a sudden or abrupt conquest. Rather, it was a stubborn step-by-step advance, requiring most of the period between 1300 and 1200 B.C.E.

The fourth book of the Bible, called *Numbers*, tells how the Israelites, led by Moses and his brother Aaron, the priest, encamped at Kadesh-Barnea in the desert of Paran southwest of the Dead Sea and south of modern Gaza. From there Moses sent out twelve scouts, one from each of the tribes, with instructions to "see what kind of land it is" and whether the people living in it were "strong or weak, few or many."

The scouts reconnoitered for forty days, then came back and reported that the land promised to the Israelites indeed did "flow with milk and honey" and bore much rich fruit. But they warned

[33]

that fierce people already lived in the land, secured in strongly fortified towns. Only two—Caleb, son of Hezron, of the tribe of Judah, and Joshua, son of Nun, of the tribe of Ephraim—urged the Israelites to move ahead and take the land. The others warned, "We cannot attack these people. They are too strong for us."

Frightened and fatigued, the Israelites began to grumble, asking, "Why is the Lord bringing us into this land . . . ? Would it not be better for us to return to Egypt?" It was even suggested that they reject Moses and pick another leader whom they would follow back to Egypt.

In despair Moses and Aaron "fell prostrate" before the assembled Israelites. They might have been stoned had not the Lord intervened. Angered by the rebelliousness of the people, the Lord proclaimed that the doubters and defeatists should die while still in the desert. Of the men over twenty, only Caleb and Joshua should enter the land assigned to Israel.

These and other Bible tales of restlessness and resentment against the leadership of Moses and Aaron doubtless dramatize the long, discouraging, step-by-step preliminaries to the conquest of Canaan by the tribes of Israel. Even Moses and Aaron, for all their inspired and stubborn faith, grew fainthearted at times.

While the Israelites were encamped at Kadesh, conditions were bad. Miriam, elder sister of Moses, died there and was buried. Water was lacking, and the people gathered to complain that both they and their herds were dying of thirst. "Why did you lead us from Egypt only to take us to this miserable place lacking grain, fruit, or even water to drink?"

Instead of facing and answering them, Moses and Aaron left the meeting. Then the Lord spoke to the despondent Moses and instructed him to strike the rock with his staff, and water would flow out for beasts and men to drink. Moses did so, and the healing waters gushed out.

However, the Lord was displeased with Moses and Aaron. He charged them with having failed on their own account to make manifest to the Israelites the power and sanctity of their God. Hence, in punishment, they should not be allowed to lead the people "into the land that I shall give them."

Efforts to break into the promised land itself began with the oasis of Kadesh as a point of departure. At first the Israelites were thwarted by forces of Canaanites marshaled under the chieftain of Arad, a center northeast of modern Beersheba. Moses then led the Israelites in the opposite direction—southeast—all the way down to the site of Eilat at the head of the Gulf of Aqaba. From there they marched northward—always well east of the great natural gash of the Jordan Valley, the Dead Sea, and the Jordan River itself—bypassing the kingdoms of Edom and Moab along the way.

Once they had crossed the Arnon River, which flows westward into the Dead Sea, they turned northwestward and repelled a resisting force of Amorites. Next they won a victory over Og, King of Bashan. This gave the Hebrews command of the plains of Moab, leading across the Jordan near where it empties into the northern end of the Dead Sea.

From this favorable position, still east of the Jordan River, the aged leader and lawgiver Moses begged his God: "Let me cross over the Jordan and see this good land, this fine hill country, and the Lebanon!"

His ardent request was refused because—according to the Bible's fifth book, *Deuteronomy*—Moses had failed to uphold the sanctity of the Lord during the critical time of water shortage at Kadesh in the desert of Zin.

Moses was permitted only to go to the top of Mount Pisgah and to gaze into the distance. "Look well, for you shall not cross the Jordan . . ." After he had looked toward the west on the land that the Lord had promised to the descendants of Abraham, Isaac, and Jacob, Moses died. He was buried in the ravine "opposite Beth-peor in the land of Moab," but the site of his burial, a few miles east of the upper end of the Dead Sea, remains undiscovered to this day.

West of the Jordan the conquest continued under Joshua of the tribe of Ephraim, a formidable man of war and actually one of the first of the so-called judges—the freely chosen tribal magistrates and leaders who had authority both in peace and in war.

The first Israelite shrine in Canaan itself was built at Gilgal near Jericho. When Jericho was captured, the Israelites moved westward and northward in the direction of the present metropolis of Tel-Aviv. A major victory was won about 1250 B.C.E. at Gibeon between modern Jerusalem and Ramla. The Gibeonites were being attacked by a league of five other Canaanite cities, each of which had its customary chieftain or "king." Joshua intervened and with his forces relieved Gibeon and drove the besiegers down the steep slopes of Mount Beth-Horon.

Thus, by taking advantage of the constant local rivalries and intrigues, the principal Israelite tribes were able before 1100 B.C.E. to occupy more or less well-defined and desirable parts of Canaan. The large tribe of Judah settled west of the Dead Sea. North of that sea lay the lands worked by the tribesmen of Ephraim and of Manasseh. Those of Naphtali settled in the upper Galilee, northwest of the Sea of Galilee, around the present site of the famous center of Safed.

The boundaries of the Israelite tribal zones were not at first rigid or static. There were extensive shifts and changes. Thus not long before 1100 B.C.E. tribesmen of Dan moved all the way from somewhat west of Jerusalem to an area considerably north of the Sea of Galilee. As they traveled they lived off the land by looting. Having conquered the Canaanite city of Laish near Mount Hermon, they gave it their own name of Dan. Later, the proverbial phrase meaning from far north to far south in Israel was "from Dan to Beersheba," much like "from rockbound Maine to sunny California" in the United States.

Even to 1100 B.C.E., the Israelite tribes held no part of the coast. This was the territory of the Philistines, a sea-oriented people who had originated in the eastern Greek islands and in what is now southern Turkey. They began coming south about 1190 B.C.E., overran the coastal areas of what is now Israel, and even seriously threatened Egypt itself. Under Pharaoh Rameses II they were forced back into Israel—but not easily. From then on they held sway along the southern coast of Israel, up to and including the site of modern Jaffa.

Philistine, the name of these conquerors-from-the-sea, led to the name *Palestine*, very often used for the entire area of present Israel and parts of Jordan. The principal cities of the Philistines were Gaza, Ashkelon, Ashdod, Ekron, and Gath.

Northward beyond the Philistine sector, on a level with Mount Hermon and about 45 miles north of the Sea of Galilee, lay the coastal territory of another important marine people: the Phoenicians-Sidonians. Their cities included Tyre, Sidon, and Byblos along the Mediterranean coast. At that time they even held the important site of the city we call Damascus.

The Israelites, on the other hand, were settled mainly in hill country farther inland and in the Trans-Jordan east of the great Jordan Valley. Their major segment was a large, somewhat irregular zone reaching south to about the middle of the Dead Sea and extending northward on both sides of the Jordan River nearly to the Sea of Galilee. West of that small sea or lake lay a little patch of territory divided among the tribesmen of Issachar, Asher, and Zebulun. North of that lake was an even smaller area held by the tribesmen of Dan.

If a traveler journeyed northward along a line about midway between the Mediterranean coast and the Jordan, he would leave the territory of the tribe of Simeon, then cross the large area of the tribe of Judah, and, after leaving Jerusalem, pass through portions of Benjamin, Ephraim, and Manasseh as he headed always northward.

On the other hand, if he traveled due north through the Trans-Jordan east of the great Jordan Valley, he would leave the territory of the tribe of Gad, pass then through portions of Reuben, then again of Gad, and finally of Manasseh.

The actual tribal-territorial divisions were neither neat nor simple. Many a later map supposed to show the divisions of the land of Israel in biblical times has oversimplified. Complications arose and readjustments took place after the early days of more or less unified conquest gave way to the later generations of settled residence as farmers, orchardists, vineyardists, and herdsmen.

Local self-government prevailed in this era, the era of the tribal judges. There was no large, dominant, or absolute central ruler or

[37]

regime, even among the "children" of Israel-Jacob. Such large, inclusive, and tyrannical regimes as those in Mesopotamia or Egypt were as yet alien to this small, varied, but desirable land so dearly beloved by the once-nomadic Hebrew tribes who had fought their way out from the desert. Here there was neither need nor opportunity for the extensive and expensive engineering and hydraulic irrigation projects that had molded the societies of Mesopotamia and Egypt.

It is not possible to state positively how many Israelites established themselves in what we now call Israel. The Bible tells of a census made at the final encampment of the Hebrew tribes before they first crossed the Jordan after the death of Moses—a census that totaled 600,000. This seems impossibly many to have wandered as a group and lived off the bitter and barren Sinai desert between Egypt and Israel. However, it is interesting to compare the relative numbers attributed to the different tribes.

First there were about 23,000 members of the special tribe of Levi. Theirs was the hereditary task of serving as priests and priestly assistants in the rituals of sacrifice, praise, and worship of the invisible one God of their people.

The remaining hundreds of thousands were divided among the tribes in about the following percentages, in order of decreasing size: Judah, 13 percent; Dan, 11 percent; Issachar, 11 percent; Zebulun, 10 percent; Asher, 9 percent; Manasseh, 9 percent; Benjamin, 8 percent; Naphtali, 7½ percent; Reuben, 7½ percent; Gad, 7 percent; Ephraim, 5½ percent; and Simeon, 4 percent.

Should we refer to these as the tribes of Israel or as the Hebrew tribes? The *Hebrews* is often used as the name for these people. It also has been used often in past centuries to apply to Jews in all parts of the world. Even today *Hebrew* is often used interchangeably with *Jew* or *Jewish*.

Hebrew is also one of the rather extensive and historically important family of languages spoken by the many Semitic peoples, who, according to the Bible and Jewish tradition, all descended from Shem, eldest son of Noah.

The Semitic languages included three main branches: the eastern, among which were the Assyrian, Babylonian, and Syriac; the southern, including Ethiopian; and—most meaningful here—the northwestern, among which were languages now called Ugaritic, Phoenician, Aramaic, and Hebrew itself.

The Aramaic language was at one time very widespread among the common people of the region. It was, in fact, the language spoken by Jesus, his disciples, and the masses of people to whom they preached.

Hebrew as a language could be called a combination of or cross between Aramaic and Phoenician. Among all these related languages, Hebrew is today the only one surviving and growing as a living tongue.

The roots linking the Hebrew language to the land called Israel are deep indeed, reaching back more than three thousand years— to the period between the time the Israelite nomads left the desert for Canaan, their "promised land," and the later days when they were firmly settled in that land and had become the subjects of unified monarchs, or kings. That in-between era is commonly called the Period of the Judges.

All through this initial period in Israel, tribe and family were extremely important. The tribe, in fact, was like a kind of enlarged and extended family. Each tribesman's or tribeswoman's duties, privileges, and rights existed largely within the tribal framework. The tribal traditions provided their constitution, their bill of rights, and sometimes even their declaration of independence. These early rural communities were to a surprising extent self-governed.

Just as individual family households were dominated by their patriarchs, so the tribal communities were ruled and regulated by their accepted elders. The Council of Elders did not include *all* the old people, or *only* old people, but persons whose influence, esteem, and standing made them preeminent in the community. There were even instances in which the Councils of Elders included women.

Not every problem could be considered and decided by a council or a council "committee." There were decisions to be made in times of peace, and plans or commands to be issued in times of warfare, which could come only from a single, accepted leader. This leader, selected by the Council of Elders, was called a "judge." Such a judge played a role rather like that of the chief of an Indian tribe. The Council of Elders, in fact, acted somewhat like the tribal council or conclave of an Indian tribe in the days of self-rule, before the white men stole their lands and disrupted their lives. An Israelite judge was chosen, supported, advised, and sometimes even deposed and replaced, by the tribal Council of Elders.

It is essential that we understand this, for what became later the Kingdom of Judah-Israel originated and arose out of this initial long period of relatively democratic self-rule and local independence.

The judges were by no means free to do as they wished. They were bound by the traditions, taboos, customs, conventions, and precedents of their tribes. They were expected to judge fairly and not to enrich themselves from their high offices. It is no wonder that tribal membership was stressed and prized by the people who settled in the land we today call Israel.

The Bible mentions by name a number of the many judges who served during this significant early era before there was a king over Israel. These included the Ephraimite Deborah, wife of Lapidoth, who lived at Mount Ephraim between Ramah and Beth-el; Othniel, son of Kenoz of Judah; Ehud, son of Gera of Benjamin; Shamgar, son of Anoth of Asher; Tola, son of Perah of Issachar; and the name best known today among all these judges—Samson, the strangely weak strong-man judge of Dan.

To the extent that there were intertribe councils and leagues, the judges represented their own tribes. In times of armed defense or aggression, the judge was expected to be the principal military leader, or at least the "chief of staff." He was also the principal recruiter and mobilizer of manpower and resources.

The position of judge was not basically hereditary, but in some cases the son or sons of a judge might succeed their father. Two such sequences are mentioned in the Bible. Gideon of Manasseh successfully led his tribesmen against camel-mounted marauders. His son Abi-melech then served as a judge and established a kind of capital between Shilo and Shechem, destroying the latter.

However, he was killed after only three years while leading the siege of another fortified Canaanite town.

Changed conditions strained the abilities of the judge-based governments of the tribes. Around 1050 B.C.E. the Philistines from their coastal strong points began to press ever harder against the Israelites to their east. Folktales tell of the great battle of Ebenezer in which the volunteer fighters of the Israelite tribal league were defeated, the famed sanctuary of Shiloh apparently was destroyed, and the most sacred single object of the Israelite religion—the Ark—was captured.

The Ark, a box of fine acacia wood less than four feet long on any side, was a portable sanctuary. Tradition says that it was lined and jacketed in gold, that its lid was shaped to resemble a divine throne, and that its ends were ornamented with figures of winged lions with human heads, which were called *cherubim* (plural of *cherub*). Golden rings on its sides made it possible to carry the Ark long distances on poles. Such portability had once been necessary, for it was believed to be the very same traveling sanctuary carried by the wandering children of Israel following their escape from bondage in Egypt.

The loss of their Ark, even though temporary, was shocking evidence of Israelite weakness in the face of growing Philistine strength. After 1050 B.C.E. the Philistines made further serious inroads. They put their own men in control as governors of centers that previously had been wholly Israelite. Philistine warriors held outposts well inside the former territory of the tribal descendants of Father Abraham. The fears of the inhabitants mounted. They and their elders clamored more and more loudly for drastic and effective changes.

It was at this crucial time that a tall, handsome Benjaminite journeyed from the house of his father, the farmer Kish in Gibeah. Some female asses from the family livestock were missing, and Saul, the son, hoped to find them and bring them safely back.

However, on the borderland between the tribal lands of Benjamin and Ephraim he found not the missing animals but something wholly and historically different. And what he brought back has become part of the immortal epic of the opening books of the Bible, the *Torah* of the children of Israel.

[41]

3

EXPANSION UNDER DAVID, SPLENDOR UNDER SOLOMON —AND A FATEFUL DIVISION

(TO ABOUT 928 B.C.E.)

When all the elders of Israel came to David in Hebron,
[he] made an agreement with them,
and they anointed him King of Israel.

David . . . reigned . . . thirty-three years
in Jerusalem over all Israel and Judah.

—II SAMUEL 5:3–5

Saul's search took place about 1025 B.C.E., and it was probably at least four hundred years later, or nearly 600 B.C.E., before the surviving folktales, legends, and chronicles were assembled into the document that became the biblical book of I Samuel. The views revealed in that far later document are colored by much that happened in the land of Israel during the centuries *after* Saul became the first king, or kinglike leader, of the children of Israel.

The man who "discovered" Saul was Samuel, a venerable judge and sage, today regarded also as an early prophet. As he grew older he appointed his two sons to help him judge his people, but as they sat in judgment at Beersheba they proved to be corrupt, selling their decisions for bribes.

Then a great gathering of elders—"all the elders of Israel"—went to Samuel, urging, "Now that you are old and your sons do not follow your example, appoint over us a king such as other nations have, to judge and lead us." The word *judge* referred to peacetime government; *lead*, however, referred to wartime command.

Samuel answered with a powerful warning against the disadvantages of the king system compared to the judge system. Remember that this book of the Bible was written hundreds of years after the fact. Obviously, with the experience of centuries of kingly rule over the Jews in the promised land, its authors were denouncing royal abuses in the light of what they themselves had seen or known.

Samuel warned that a king would draft or conscript their sons for military service, or even for menial tasks such as "to run before his chariot." Their daughters too would be taken to serve as cooks and bakers for the king and his standing army. A king would establish forced labor under his own overseers and gang bosses. The people—formerly free farmers, herdsmen, orchardists— would be forced to cultivate and harvest the royal estates. They would be obliged to make weapons for the king, and to supply food for his court and armies from their own produce. Even the landworkers who served in their fields would no longer be available, for they would be taken to work the king's lands.

Samuel delivered an eloquent warning against the evils of royal despotism, especially those aspects that much later were called "taxation without representation." Finally, he predicted, "You yourselves shall be slaves to the king. Then you will cry out . . ." But that outcry, he warned, would come too late.

Among several antimonarchist passages in the Bible, none seems today more timely or eloquent than this. And Samuel's advice was really the advice of God himself—as the book of I Samuel makes quite clear. But it made no difference. This self-willed stubborn people would not be swayed. "No," their elders answered, "we must have a king to rule over us, so that we may be like the other nations—a king who will rule us and lead us in war and fight our battles."

When Samuel consulted God again, the Lord reminded him, "It is not you whom they reject. They are rejecting me as their king . . . deserting me and worshipping strange gods." Yet finally God told Samuel to inform the elders that their demand for a king would be granted.

When tall, handsome Saul appeared to ask after the lost asses, Samuel greeted him as God's choice for the new kingship. Saul was then anointed, and Samuel declared that it would be his task to save Israel from its enemies.

Saul had no palace, no treasury, no royal court. He was plowing as usual behind a yoke of oxen when the first crisis arose: the Ammonites were besieging the Israelite city of Jabesh. Cutting a pair of oxen into bits, Saul sent the fragments throughout Israel by messengers on a mobilizing mission, warning, "If anyone fails to follow Saul, the same will be done to his oxen."

The Bible tells of an enormous response, including 70,000 men of Judah and 300,000 of Israel. (This Bible chronicle was written at a time when there were two Hebrew kingdoms—Judah to the south, Israel to the north.)

In a surprise attack Saul scattered the Ammonites and saved the city of Jabesh. To the many in Israel who before had scoffed at his ability to be a real leader and king, Saul showed mercy. He was anointed again to full kingship at Gilgal, the first religious center of the Israelites in Canaan.

Saul retained two thousand picked men and put one thousand more under his brave son Jonathan, who proceeded to overwhelm the Philistine garrison in Gibeah. Saul proclaimed the new victory throughout the land. The Philistines, who had assembled in strength to strike down this new military threat from the Israelites, were scattered by the forces under Saul and Jonathan and driven toward their coastal centers.

For about nineteen years in all, Saul was the single leader of the Israelites. He is called the first king, but actually he was more like an inspired and supreme "judge." His old home in Gibeah served as his makeshift capital, and he chose most of his assistants and officers from the men of his own tribe of Benjamin.

With this very restricted kind of kingship, Saul managed to win battles against nomadlike enemies such as the Ammonites and the Amalekites, but he was unable to strike really decisive blows against the far stronger Philistines to the west.

A time came when Saul could not make his policies and decisions prevail among even his own "subjects." One shrewd, gifted, and endlessly ambitious aide to Saul was a young man from Bethlehem in the tribal region of Judah: David, son of Jesse. About 1010 B.C.E. in a fabulous one-to-one combat, David felled and killed Goliath, a formidable champion of the Philistines. Later, David married a daughter of Saul and became a dear friend of Saul's son Jonathan.

After a time Saul and David, once very close, became estranged, and David sought refuge in the Judean desert, a favorite hiding place for rebels and outlaws. In its caves and sheltered crevices he gathered around him other outlaws and rootless men like himself. They became a sort of private army of professional fighters, feared and respected by the Jewish inhabitants of the region. Saul sought more than once to capture and punish David. But the Bible tells of dramatic episodes in which, when it came to final choice, each showed mercy to the other.

David finally went all the way in his opposition and, with his gang, became an open renegade, taking service with Achish, king of Gath, an enemy of Saul and the Israelites. Achish assigned to David as his base the town of Ziklag, about midway between modern Gaza and Beersheba. There David and his freebooter force helped the Philistines by attacks on the Amalekites, raiders from the desert. David took care to increase his personal popularity among the elders of the tribes of Judah and Simeon by sharing with them booty taken in his raids.

David's private troop came to include malcontents not only from Judah and Benjamin but also from alien non-Jewish tribes such as the Ammonites and the Hittites.

Internal tensions arose, prevailing for about four years, 1010 to 1006 B.C.E. Saul was meanwhile forced to deal with the principal external threat, the Philistines. A great showdown struggle drew near. Philistine forces mobilized at Aphek, about ten miles east of Jaffa. Then they marched north and east, encamping at Shemen less than twenty miles from the Sea of Galilee. Saul led his forces to the top of Mount Gilboa nearby. On the night before the battle he sought the aid of a spirit medium, a witch at En-dor. In disguise, he persuaded her to summon up the dead Samuel, the judge and prophet.

Samuel, protesting against being brought back to the world of the living, told Saul that disaster awaited: "By tomorrow you and your sons will be with me, and the Lord will have delivered the army of Israel into the hands of the Philistines."

Indeed, the next day brought dire defeat to the Israelite forces, with death to Saul and three of his sons. The immediate result was that for the time being the Philistines dominated the towns of the rich valley of Jezreel near the scene of the battle.

Abner, Saul's chief captain, had, however, managed to escape. He set up a center of government at Mahanaim, on the opposite, or eastern, side of the Jordan River, and there he proclaimed Esh-baal, a surviving son of Saul, as the new king.

At this point David gave up his sanctuary with the Philistines and returned to his homeland of Judah with his well-trained band of outlaw fighters. Settled at Hebron, he loudly proclaimed his personal grief over the deaths of Saul and Jonathan. Just prior to the battle of Gilboa, however, David and his men had joined with the Philistine forces and would have been fighting against Saul and his sons but for the fact that the Philistine lords did not trust David quite enough to send him and his company into battle against the men of Israel.

At Hebron, David wooed and won the support of the elders of Judah, and they agreed to acclaim him as king. For the next seven or eight years Hebron remained his base and capital while he maneuvered and fought successfully to expand his control.

Israel was now, and not for the last time, split between two rival and antagonistic kings. Finally the forces of David and Esh-baal met in battle. At the Pool of Gibeon, David's experienced raiders defeated the army loyal to Esh-baal. A complex series of plots and countermoves followed. Within two years David had brought about the deaths of both Esh-baal and Abner, commander of Esh-baal's army. Then David invited to Hebron the elders of the tribes that had been ruled by Esh-baal, persuading them finally to accept him as their new king.

Thus, by the age of about thirty-three, the Judean adventurer David had become the king of Judah to the south, and ruler also of what was to be known later as the Kingdom of Israel, to the north.

Between the two regions of David's royal rule, like a thorn in the side of his new kingships, projected the small but importantly situated region of the Jebusites, a Canaanite people. Its center was a beautifully located hill town then known as Jebus, earlier known as Salem. About 1000 B.C.E. David's seasoned warriors besieged and took it. He began with little delay to convert it into the king's own capital and center of rule. It was a move typical of his shrewd imagination. This new royal town belonged to none of the tribal territories. David thus began his new unified kingship outside the traditional tribal patterns and free from some of their inevitable jealousies. Jebus soon became known as *Yerushalayim* (Jerusalem), and also as "the city of David," destined to become one of the most famous and influential city names and concepts in all human history.

His new city had to be defended from the start. The Philistine overlords in their fortified coastal centers had taken alarm. They saw the threat in this latest move by the adventurer who had once served their policies against Israel. But their countermeasures came too late. David's formidable fighters twice beat back Philistine columns sent against Jerusalem and chased them shamefully past Gibeah, halfway to the coast of the Mediterranean.

It was the beginning of the end of Philistine power on the coastal strip between Israel and the sea. Soon David had confined the Philistines to a restricted zone extending some sixty miles along the coast and only ten to fifteen miles inland. It included the sites of the present Israeli cities of Ashdod, Ashkelon, and Gaza. Somewhat north of Ashdod, the Hebrew tribesmen of Dan held a coastal zone which included the sites of modern Jaffa and Tel-Aviv. Thus David gained harbor and water transport facilities to bring into his territory imported products from far outside the limits of his rapidly growing realm.

Swiftly and effectively his forces struck also southeast and northeast of Jerusalem. First he conquered the Moabites east of the Dead Sea, then the Ammonites northeast of it. Later his warriors plunged farther north, and less than fifty miles east of the Sea of Galilee they defeated a coalition headed by the Aramean ruler of what is now Syria. Thence they moved to Damascus itself, where they garrisoned the city.

King David was by this time supreme in the Trans-Jordan. Also, in the far south below the Dead Sea, he defeated the Edomites, whose ruler fled the length of the Sinai peninsula to seek shelter in Egypt.

During more than a score of years, ending with his death in 968 B.C.E., David ruled or controlled a region vast in area even by

[50]

modern standards. From Eilat in the far south to the Euphrates River near Aleppo, Syria, his sway was either directly or indirectly supreme. He had his numerous Israelite subjects in the twin, united kingdoms. He had subjugated or enslaved outsiders who owed him labor services. And he demanded and received tribute from defeated monarchs who were allowed to rule on so long as they did not fall behind in their heavy payments to this dynamic man of war in his palace on the Jerusalem hill called Mount Zion.

Of prime importance was David's total control over both of the great transportation routes and their various branches—the Way by the Sea (*Via Maris*), and the King's Highway east of the Jordan. Caravans could cross his great territory only with his permission and after payment of the required fees to his officers.

With the coastal land of the Phoenicians or Sidonians in the western part of present-day Lebanon, David enjoyed a close and mutually beneficial relationship. Hiram, the canny king of Tyre, was never molested. He was too helpful as a source of lumber from his Lebanese forests, and of other supplies needed for the royal designs of David.

Saul had had almost none of the machinery of rule. David had a great deal, and it grew as the years passed. The dour warnings of Samuel came true. David taxed his subjects heavily; he maintained a large standing army, a military caste, and a considerable number of overseers, stewards, and scribes for his large and rich private estates.

His rocketlike rise to power and dominance over such a great region was due partly to his personal talents, but also to the important fact that during this time both Egypt on the one side and the Mesopotamian regions on the other had no effective counterpower to check him. This was an oft-repeated picture. Only when no single overwhelming military power existed in either the valley of the Nile or the Tigris-Euphrates valley could an extensive, expansive, and formidable Israel arise and continue to exist.

David is better remembered today as a musician, a poet, and a worshipper of Yahweh, the invisible one God of the Israelites, than as a general, diplomat, and administrator of empire. At the same time that his Jerusalem-based officials weakened the influence and roles of the old traditional tribes, he found a new and alluring way to fire the enthusiasm of his subjects and focus it on the city of David itself. With a brilliant flair for the dramatic, he arranged a spectacular procession and celebration to bring the Ark of the Covenant in glory for the first time to Jerusalem from the northern Benjaminite sanctuary where it had been in safekeeping. Tens of thousands of Israelites marched, headed by David himself, who danced and sang in jubilation before the ox-drawn cart that brought this most sacred object to the tent that had been prepared to house it at Jerusalem.

Great numbers of beasts were sacrificed on traditional altars. There was much feasting, and it was ordained that Jerusalem was thenceforward to be the one great cult shrine for the entire realm. Officiating at the new tabernacle was Asaph as high priest, aided by nine lesser priests and some seventy guardians or gatekeepers. Incense burning and elaborate choral music were also part of the continuous ritual of prayer and praise at the tabernacle, in whose Holy of Holies the Ark now reposed.

Despite the many glories of his reign, David's rule made life bitter for great numbers of his subjects. Increasingly, many common people and the elders of the tribes resented the incessant and growing exactions from Jerusalem. Their resistance sometimes interfered with the plans of the king himself. Thus, for example, their refusal to cooperate made it impossible to carry through the complete census that he had ordered as a basis for further taxation and crop contributions from his subjects.

In his later years a series of outright rebellions demonstrated the extent of the bitterness. Absalom, one of David's favorites among his many sons and daughters by numerous wives, sought to unseat his father about the year 978 B.C.E. Absalom's supporters included even members of David's own tribe, Judah.

After the revolt was crushed and Absalom killed, David appears to have tried to win back the loyalty of his leaders in Judah, but his favored treatment of them only served to generate resentment among the many northern tribes. An attempted uprising took place under Sheba, a Benjaminite leader. David survived this crisis also, but found that his only real support this time came from the tribe of Judah. The northern tribes had become alienated from his rule.

With advancing age, David became more dictatorial and more easily swayed by lust. Among his many wives his favorite came to be Bathsheba, whom he had stolen, in a scandalous abuse of power, from one of his loyal mercenaries, Uriah the Hittite, whose death he had then arranged.

Solomon, precocious young son of Bathsheba and David, was by no means the eldest heir, but after a series of secret and unworthy palace intrigues it was Solomon who was anointed as the future king, with the consent of his declining father.

When David died, Solomon began his rule. Though still in his teens, he proved as ruthless in getting rid of rivals as any older prince could have been. In making a clean sweep of all but his closest supporters, he replaced Joab, David's top general, with Benaiah and ousted Abiathar, high priest of the tabernacle, to make way for his own man, Zadok.

Solomon reigned for about forty years, 968 to 928 B.C.E., during which time totally different policies prevailed in the "promised land." He turned from military campaigns to peaceful consolidation and commercial activities. Material splendor was his personal preference, and also part of his program to impress other monarchs in the great world outside. "Solomon in all his glory" became a byword and the source of many a folktale and legend. The biblical book of I Kings recalls that "Solomon ruled over all the land west of the Euphrates from Tiphsah to Gaza and over all its kings, and he had peace on all his borders. . . . Thus Judah and Israel lived in security, every man under his vine or his fig tree, from Dan to Beersheba."

Solomon's marriages, more numerous even than those of David, were largely diplomatic rather than personal affairs. He cemented firmer relations with various monarchs and men of importance by adding them to the ranks of his many fathers-in-law. Most notable was his winning as wife an Egyptian princess, daughter of the reigning pharaoh. With Egypt to the southwest and Tyre to the north, Solomon long enjoyed cooperative and profitable trade relations and treaties of friendship. Even the Queen of Sheba came from far south to discuss matters of trade with him.

In keeping with his imperial concept of rule, Solomon transformed Jerusalem into an imposing capital, far different from the small and rather modest city of his father. Here he built his costly, ornate palaces, courts, halls of administration, harems, stables, and guard garrisons.

Most famous and influential of all his building projects was the first permanent Temple, replacing the traditional tent-tabernacle. Placed on Jerusalem's hill called Mount Moriah, almost as a part of his own group of royal buildings, it was designed to serve as the sole cult and worship center for all the children of Israel under his rule.

Daily offerings of incense and spices were made at the Temple. In the Temple courtyard, east of its bronze gates on a great brazen altar, animals were offered up as sacrifices also, as was common among the religions of that ancient world. Blood, fire, and cleansing water were prominent elements in these sacrifices. There were milder rituals also, including choral singing and chanting in praise of the one God.

The Temple was not a house to be used by worshippers in the sense of a modern synagogue or church. It was rather the private sanctuary of God himself, into which only the ordained priests were admitted so that they might carry out approved and prescribed rituals on behalf of the people as a whole. On various well-known holidays, people might gather outside the Temple in courtyards assigned for that purpose, but they were not permitted to enter the sanctuary itself. However, all adult males were expected to contribute to the maintenance of the Temple—with either money or farm produce. Thus were maintained the high priest, his staff of assistant priests, the singers, caretakers, guards, and other Temple officials.

According to the Bible description, the interior of the Temple of Solomon was richly carved and decorated. From east to west its three main chambers were increasingly holy. At the western end was the last and smallest, the "holy of holies," into which the high priest entered but once each year. Here was enshrined the small but deeply venerated Ark, the portable case that David had accompanied to Jerusalem. This most sacred receptacle came ultimately to be called "the Ark of the Covenant," and the tradition arose that it contained three extraordinary relics: First, the remains of the same stone tablets that Moses had brought down from Mount Sinai bearing the Ten Commandments; second, a pot of manna, the miraculous food on which the Israelites had fed during their desert wanderings; and finally, the rod of Aaron, brother of Moses and founder of the priestly line of Israel. Thus in the most sacred part of the Temple were enshrined the divine laws handed down to govern the lives of men on earth.

Later folktales and legends depicted the rule of Solomon as a kind of golden age. The population of the land of Israel apparently did increase impressively during this extended era without wars and invasions, reaching some 800,000, or about double the size it had been when Saul became a first central chieftain, called a king.

Another side of Solomon's era seems a good deal less attractive. His reign was costly to his people in taxes and also in forced labor, which for the first time was imposed on his own subjects as well as on slaves and bondservants taken by conquest. His administrators paid little attention to old tribal boundaries and traditions. The northern tribes especially felt themselves slighted and abused.

The new aristrocracy of courtiers, diplomats, and bureaucrats grew larger in Jerusalem and in the lesser centers of government. The prophecies voiced by Samuel regarding the social disadvantages of being ruled by a king applied to the period of Solomon even more than to that of David, his father.

Because of the discontent of his people, the last years of Solomon's reign were dark ones, despite his superficial splendors and the honors accorded him by subservient courtiers and charioted men-at-arms.

In time a more aggressive new pharaoh, Shishak, became ruler in Egypt, ending the era of Israel's good relations with that important neighbor. Pressure from Egypt increased. Solomon sought to offset it by added expenditures for defense. Finally he had so drained his resources that he was obliged to turn over—really, to sell—a score of towns in the Galilee to the canny king of Tyre.

Among the overseers of Solomon's forced labor draft of the northern tribes was Jeroboam of the tribe of Ephraim. Encouraged by another Ephraimite, the prophet or agitator Abijah, Jeroboam instigated an uprising. When it failed, he found refuge with Pharaoh Shishak, who was always interested in aiding opposition to Solomon.

When Solomon died in 928 B.C.E., his appointed and anointed successor was his son Rehoboam, then about forty, who had grown up amidst the splendors and snobberies of the Jerusalem court. The great region of Judah accepted him as king without delay, but he found that he would have to secure the approval also of the northern tribes, who had earlier separately agreed to accept his grandfather David as their monarch.

At Shechem, some thirty-five miles north of Jerusalem, and within the administrative district named for the old tribe of Ephraim, a great confrontation took place. At this old center of Canaanite and early Israelite worship were gathered elders from the remaining tribes other than Judah: Ephraim, Issachar, Zebulun, Naphtali, and the rest. Their mood was grim and demanding. They told Rehoboam that they would accept him as their king *if* he pledged to do away with the past burdens and abuses they had suffered under Solomon.

Rehoboam's background apparently had ill-prepared him to cope with such defiance. He asked for three days in which to reply, then consulted the two contrasting advisory councils who were with him. The venerable Council of Elders (who had sometimes advised Solomon) urged him to give a reassuring reply, for if he did, they said, these people "will be your faithful servants." The other group, consisting of young palace aristocrats, including, almost certainly, many of his half-brothers and the companions of his youth, reflected the arrogance of an imperial regime. They urged him to defy and humiliate these upstart protestors. So Rehoboam flung in the faces of the spokesmen of the northern tribes a most divisive and derisive reply: "My father made your burden heavy, but I shall add to that burden. My father lashed you with whips, but I shall lash you with scorpions!"

The outraged representatives at once withdrew from the parley, denouncing their ties to the dynasty of David and warning, "Now look to your own house . . ." Thus the covenant their forebears had made with David in Hebron was, at Shechem, cancelled in Rehoboam's face. The traditions and loyalties of the Hebrew tribes were obviously not yet extinct, even though they had been much weakened during the reigns of David and Solomon.

Rehoboam tried to send a spokesman to change their minds, but they stoned and killed this emissary. Rehoboam himself barely managed to escape by chariot to his palace in Jerusalem.

Meanwhile, the fugitive Jeroboam returned from the sanctuary provided by the Egyptian ruler Shishak and was accepted as king by the elders of the northern tribes, thenceforth to be called "the Kingdom of Israel." Rehoboam's smaller remnant to the south became "the Kingdom of Judah," named for the tribe whose lands made up most of its small area.

The Bible tells that Rehoboam mobilized 180,000 men from Judah and Benjamin, intending to force the northerners to accept his rule, but a seer or prophet warned him in the name of the Lord, "You must not . . . fight against your brother Israelites. Let every man return home. . . ."

4

DEFEAT, DISAPPEARANCE, AND THE FIRST RETURN

(TO ABOUT 332 B.C.E.)

By the waters of Babylon, we sat down,
    yes, we wept when we remembered Zion.
We hung up our harps on the willow trees. . . .

. . . They who carried us away captives
    required of us a song . . . saying
"Sing us one of the songs of Zion."

How shall we sing the Lord's song
    in a strange land?
If I forget you, O Jerusalem,
    let my right hand forget its cunning.
If I do not remember you,
    let my tongue cleave to the roof of my mouth;
    if I do not prefer Jerusalem above my chief joy.

—FROM PSALM 137

The separations and rivalries thus begun lasted a long time, a period often called the age of "the divided monarchy." It endured, with many variations and complications, from 928 until just after 600 B.C.E., or about 330 years (nearly as long as from the beginning of the Hebrew tribes' conquest of Canaan to the death of King Solomon).

It was a period of terrible weaknesses, yet also of great accomplishments. Among them was the completion of the documents which, after various revisions, evolved into the principal books later chosen for inclusion in the Jewish Bible, or Old Testament.

Rulers of the two separated kingdoms turned more and more to the building of defensive fortifications and to the making of alliances with powers outside, seeking thus to compensate for their weaknesses. Meanwhile, both in Egypt and in the Mesopotamian river valleys, regimes were arising with commanders and armies far more formidable than any that had threatened either David or Solomon.

In the first years of the reign of Rehoboam over Judah, his shrunken kingdom was invaded by fierce Libyan and Ethiopian soldiers sent by the Pharaoh Shishak. They forced their way into Jerusalem and plundered treasure from the Temple, then moved on north into the new Kingdom of Israel, taking heavy toll there too. King Jeroboam's past association with the pharaoh provided him no protection now. By the time the Egyptian fighters had left with their booty, a terrible truth had been revealed: The "promised land" was vulnerable to attack by aggressive outside powers.

Seeking to build his strength and prestige, King Jeroboam revived the old religious sanctuaries and cult centers in his territory in an attempt to divert his subjects' attention and loyalty from the famous Temple of Solomon in Jerusalem, the capital of the southern and rival Kingdom of Judah.

During the period of divided kingdoms many alien religious rites and even outright idolatries were imported into both kingdoms, a result principally of the repeated efforts of their monarchs to win new alliances with outside powers. A common way to demonstrate loyalty to such alien rulers was publicly to approve and practice their religions and to offer sacrifices to their particular gods or goddesses. The Bible is full of denunciations of rulers in both kingdoms who had abandoned *Yahweh* or Jehovah, the invisible one God of their ancestors, to serve false gods.

This was not an entirely new practice. Solomon had permitted his foreign-born wives to worship in the manner of the cities or tribes from which they had come. Hence, almost within the shadow of his famous Temple had appeared chapels and sanctuaries of gods considered abominable by later Jewish prophets. However, Solomon had been strong enough to maintain in his own Temple the traditional forms of worship of his Hebrew subjects.

In seesaw wars of brother against brother, various royal regimes in Judah and Israel tried to extend their holdings in the land of Benjamin, which became a kind of arena between the two kingdoms. One king of Israel, Joash, even fought his way into Jerusalem itself, captured the king of Judah, and tore down some of the walls built to protect the sacred city of David. But neither he nor any other among nearly forty kings who sat on one or another of the two thrones tried to unite permanently the divided realms.

An interlude of relative sanity and peace was provided under two kings, Jeroboam II of Israel and Uzziah of Judah. Each extended his own territory, but never at the expense of the other. By about 750 B.C.E. Uzziah was able to pierce the coastal strip held by the Philistines and to win a segment of territory along the

Mediterranean. He conquered Edom to the east and established fortifications on the road to the southern extremity today called Eilat. Even more important, he helped to make agriculture more productive and thus more profitable for his people. Yet for some reason he seems to have drawn down on himself the resentment and hatred of the priests who headed the Temple.

About 750 B.C.E. ominous news came down from the north. In the powerful region of Assyria a bold and ruthless ruler had gained control: Tiglath-Pileser III. He had conquered all that seemed worth holding in the Fertile Crescent, down to the Persian Gulf itself.

In Israel, closer to Assyria than is Judah, fierce inner conflicts flared between those who favored alliance with, or even surrender to, Assyria, and those who held out for resistance with the help of some outside power such as Egypt. Kings who went along with one side were assassinated and replaced by advocates of the other.

The Kingdom of Judah was similarly plagued. In Jerusalem the eloquent and poetic agitator-prophet Isaiah preached powerfully against any move that might bring the vengeance of Assyria crashing down on the land and its people.

By 733 B.C.E. such cautions or precautions were too late. Tiglath-Pileser, the Assyrian monarch, had captured Damascus, killed its king, and carried away its leading citizens. Everything north of the Kingdom of Israel was in the cruel hands of the Assyrians. Their warriors then drove deep into Israel, taking Gilead and most of the Galilee. A pro-Assyrian king was hastily placed on the throne of Israel, but the threat to Israel did not end.

When Tiglath-Pileser died, his rule was taken over by Shalmaneser V. An attempt by the king of Israel to escape the yoke of Assyria was punished by a three-year siege of the city of Samaria, then the capital of the northern Jewish kingdom. Sargon, the next Assyrian monarch, finally wiped out Israel as a kingdom and destroyed the tribal identities of its people by deporting masses of them to other parts of the sprawling Assyrian empire. Thus was created the so-called mystery of "the ten lost tribes of Israel."

Most of these exiled Israelites seem to have been absorbed into the populations among which they were scattered. At the same time, the Assyrians brought into the Kingdom of Israel many non-Israelite peoples from elsewhere in their empire. Jewish family solidarities, customs, and religious practices were modified by those of the new arrivals. Because of this enforced mixing, the people of this region, later known as Samaritans, were looked on with disfavor and contempt by the Jews who lived farther south and whose ancestors had escaped the Assyrian reshuffling of the defeated peoples.

Assyrian governors ruled new provinces called Samaria and Megiddo, the latter being to the north of Samaria and west of the Jordan and the Sea of Galilee. The vanishing of the tribes of Israel made an indelible impression on the remaining Jews in the land we today call Israel. Fear stalked the towns and villages of the small kingdom of Judah. Assyrian border guards now stood within ten or fifteen miles of the walls of Jerusalem itself. Hezekiah, king of Judah, was pulled in two directions, as had been the last rulers of Israel before the catastrophe. Isaiah continued to preach against any Egyptian alliance that would antagonize Assyria. There were others, however, who urged just such an alliance as the only way to avoid the awful fate of the Kingdom of Israel. Finally, Hezekiah decided to join an anti-Assyrian revolt that included also the rulers of distant Babylon, a rebellious subject of the Assyrian empire.

Under King Sennacherib the Assyrians marched to Jerusalem, crushing the Kingdom of Tyre on their way. In vain Hezekiah sought to buy them off with rich tribute. Jerusalem was surrounded. Yet Isaiah still dared predict that the Assyrians would not enter the sacred city. Suddenly and mysteriously Sennacherib broke off the siege and left. It may be that some pestilence attacked his troops and forced this action. In any event, the pious worshippers in Judah were sure they had been saved by the Lord himself. As a matter of fact, the Kingdom of Judah survived long enough to see the breakup of the Assyrian empire, which was torn asunder by a coalition of Babylonians, Medes, and Scythians between 614 and 610 B.C.E.

Judah consolidated its gains and even expanded during the reign of King Josiah, 628–609 B.C.E. Josiah managed to reunite much of the territory once ruled by King David. Josiah restored and reformed the official Jewish worship in his land. He and his priests insisted on the sole supremacy of the Jerusalem Temple in all aspects of worship and sacrifice. The scope and strictness of these reforms are seen in the Bible book of *Deuteronomy*, which was a product of his period and policies.

Egypt's Pharaoh Neco, seeking to gain from the breakup of Assyria, invaded the Kingdom of Judah and marched northward along its coastal plain. Near what is now Haifa, Josiah was killed as his forces fought to halt the invading Egyptians. Neco then selected a son of Josiah to rule Judah in a manner agreeable to him. But not long afterward, still another conqueror arrived from that other fertile area off to the north and east. This was Nebuchadnezzar, ruler of Babylon. He twice defeated the Egyptians and finally drove them back into the Sinai peninsula itself.

Mighty Babylon now dominated the Fertile Crescent, down to the very margins of the Nile Valley. But in Judah, King Jehoiakim tried to escape this new imperial yoke, though warned against the effort by the prophet Jeremiah and others. Nebu-chadnezzar struck a series of blows as punishment. First he sent in his subject armies of Syrians, Moabites, and Ammonites against Judah. Then he moved in his own much-feared forces. Again Jerusalem was besieged, and again it was taken. The city and its Temple were plundered by the victors.

Seeking to destroy the roots from which future revolts might spring, the Babylonians rounded up ten or twelve thousand of the elite of the land and exiled them to the region around distant Babylon itself. In this and following waves of forced migration Judah lost most of its aristocrats, priestly families, leading scholars, and craftsmen.

Yet by 588 B.C.E. the next king of Judah, Zedekiah, again sought with Egyptian aid to throw off the shackles of Babylon. This time the Babylonians brought with them as allies also the fierce Edomites of the east. They took town after town, finally destroying and burning as much as they could of Jerusalem itself, including King Solomon's Temple. The destruction of the Temple was later identified with the ninth day of the Hebrew month of *Ab* or *Av*, which has become a day of Jewish mourning and lamentation.

In 587 and again in 582 B.C.E. additional numbers of select prisoners were marched off toward Babylon. This came to be called "the Babylonian captivity" of the children of Israel—another time of trial and endurance for descendants of the Hebrews who long before had survived and escaped bondage in Egypt.

Jerusalem, ravaged now and in ruins, was not even kept as the site from which the Babylonians governed what was left of the population. Instead the new governor, Gedaliah, took up his tasks at Mizpah, where he was subsequently murdered by desperately anti-Babylonian Jews. Then, fearing for their lives, numbers of Jewish resistance fighters fled all the way to Egypt. There they and their descendants served the pharaohs as professional defense troops—foreign legions, so to speak—in several strategic posts.

Though the "promised land" was not deprived of all its people, it had been stripped of all but "the poorest sort," to use a biblical phrase. Estates and orchards whose owners were now in exile were taken over by the poor who still remained or by settlers who moved in from outside regions such as Edom. Within a couple of days' journey southward from Jerusalem could now be found settlements of the so-called Idumeans. They had moved into that section from Edom itself, still farther south and east from the Dead Sea.

The great Babylonian exile in its various phases lasted from before 590 to 539 B.C.E. It was the first major scattering, or *Diaspora*, of Jews whose identity as Jews was not lost in the process. It was to be but the first of many such scatterings, mostly enforced but sometimes voluntary by people in search of greater prosperity and a better chance in life.

The former citizens of the Kingdom of Judah for the most part seem to have adjusted themselves to conditions they found in the rural regions beside "the waters of Babylon" to which they were exiled. Some became merchants, skilled craftsmen, scribes, stewards, or even financiers. They were not completely cut off from

[66]

information about their former homes in the "promised land." To their sorrow and resentment they learned from time to time how their former properties had been taken over by "squatters" and outsiders.

One of the most noted Jewish exiles in the Babylon region was the eloquent Ezekiel. His longings for a new and ideal "promised land" were voiced in his prophetic verses. They pictured a resplendent and enlarged Temple rebuilt within a land of Israel unbelievably glorified, cleansed, and redeemed. His imaginary Israel was arranged in a neat sequence from south to north to provide a parcel of land for each of the twelve tribes in this order: Gad, Zebulun, Issachar, Simeon, Benjamin, Judah, Reuben, Ephraim, Manasseh, Naphtali, Asher, and finally Dan.

Jerusalem was to be nestled between Benjamin and Judah. This imagined Israel, from Gad to Dan, was to be fertile, blessed, beauteous, and above all ample in area, for it was to take in also the onetime kingdom of Damascus. From south to north it would extend some 300 miles or more. The chief gem in its crown would be a new, vastly more imposing Temple to replace the first one, which had been so shamefully destroyed.

In reality, the turning point toward a very different future came less than a quarter century after Nebu-chadnezzar died in 562 B.C.E. By 539 new and dynamic conquerors—the Persians and their allies—were at the very gates of Babylon, whose sun of power had begun to sink. Cyrus was the military genius who had led the Persians to dominate enormous regions east and north of what was still held by Babylon.

The final fall of Babylon was swift and dramatic. Cyrus thus gained control of the entire Fertile Crescent, and Persian power extended finally from Egypt to the southwest all the way to India on the east. This empire was divided into one hundred and twenty provinces, or *medinah*, each with its own pasha or *peha*. One province was called *Yehud*. It was a part of the district, or *satrapy*, of Eber-Nahara. Yehud was the land of the Jews.

Cyrus showed a religious tolerance rare in those days, or indeed since. His subjects were permitted, perhaps even encouraged, to worship their traditional city and tribal gods, so long as their taxes and tributes were paid and they did not conspire against their

Persian overlords. Cyrus also made it possible for peoples exiled by the Babylonians to return to their old homelands.

Some but by no means all of the exiles from Judah took advantage of the chance to return to the land we now call Israel. One group of those who returned was led by a Jewish aristocrat called Shesh-bazar or Shen-azzar, probably a son of the former King Jehoiakim. With him went his nephew Zerub-babel, and Jeshua or Joshua, member of a Levite family associated in the past with the high priesthood of the Temple.

About 537 B.C.E. this company finally reached the site of Jerusalem. No joyful welcome greeted them there. The population of "remainers" was suspicious, even resentful, of those unfamiliar "returners." Judah or Yehud seemed a weak and withered remnant, and Jerusalem a mockery of what it once had been.

No Temple had existed since the great destruction of 587 B.C.E. Conditions now were so unfavorable that it was not until about twenty-two years after the first return—or 515 B.C.E.—that a substitute Temple could be completed and dedicated by the returners. It was small and unimpressive, but the traditional rituals of sacrifice, praise, and worship were once again resumed.

About sixty-five years after this "second Temple" had been dedicated, another descendant of the exiled Jews of Judah returned to Jerusalem. His name was Nehemiah, and he came with express authority from the Persian monarch, then named Artaxerxes II or III. Nehemiah found Jerusalem in a sad, even shocking state, scantily populated, its people mostly poor, unhappy, and oppressed by a few rich exploiters.

Nehemiah surrounded Jerusalem with defensive walls. The religious practices at the Temple he regarded as inadequate and indifferent. Aided by an active priest and scribe named Ezra, he forced through many religious reforms and tried to better the condition of the common people. He brought in new settlers, provided housing, and put pressure on the rich to be less greedy.

During this era of Persian rule there was no Jewish king. The high priest served generally as chief representative of his people in dealings with the Persian-appointed governors and other officials of the monarch, whose seat of government was in faraway Susa or Sushan.

5

FROM ALEXANDER, THE GREAT HELLENE, TO THE HASMONEAN "HAMMERERS"

(TO ABOUT 67 B.C.E.)

. . . Alexander the Macedonian . . . defeated Darius, King of the Persians and Medes, [and] became king in his place. . . . [Alexander] fought many campaigns, captured fortresses, and put kings to death. He advanced to the ends of the earth. . . .

. . . Alexander had reigned 12 years when he died . . . his officers took over his kingdom, each in his own territory. . . . They put on royal crowns, and so did their sons after them for many years, causing much distress over the earth.

—I MACCABEES 1:1-8

5

FROM ALEXANDER
THE GREAT HELLENE,
TO THE
HASMONEAN
"HAMMERS"

This era of return, transition, and partial reform came to a significant end in the year 332 B.C.E. The man who effected the great changeover here and in most of the rest of the known world was a genius named Alexander of Macedon (356–323 B.C.E.), better known as Alexander the Great. Youthful, endlessly active, energetic and imaginative, he had led his hardened Macedonian troops in a clean sweep of former Persian strongholds in Asia Minor, and finally (in 333 B.C.E.) had overwhelmed the Persian monarch Darius III at Issus near modern Aleppo.

Alexander's triumphal march along the coast of what today is Israel was punctuated by pauses to besiege and destroy important cities. By the winter of 332 B.C.E., he and his forces were safe in Egypt. He never entered Jerusalem itself, though several endlessly repeated legends tell of his friendly meeting with one of two different high priests of the Temple there.

Alexander became the first "western" conqueror in the promised land. His short, meteoric life, which ended in 323 B.C.E., opened that part of the world to a new social, economic, and cultural pattern, often called "hellenism" or "hellenization," for it was Greek in quality without being specifically connected with Greece in the narrower geographical sense of that word. The "promised land" was never to be quite the same after the sudden appearance and the untimely death of the great Alexander. Though a Macedonian, he brought Grecian influences into the Middle East.

His astounding empire, including just about all of the known

ALEXANDER'S CONQUES[T]

THRACE

MACEDONIA

Pella

MYSIA

Parmenid

PHRYGIA

Gordium

Ancyra

CAPPADOCIA

LYDIA

Sardis

Athens

Ephesus

Sparta

CILICIA

Miletus

LYCIA

Tarsus

Phaselis

Myriandrus

Ale

CRETE

CYPRUS

Aradus

Mediterranean Sea

Byblos

SY

Sidon

Tyre

Damo

Acre
(Acco)

Dora

Joppa

PALESTINE

Paretonium

Alexandria

Gaza

Jerusalem

Pelusium

NABATEANS

Ammonium

Memphis

EGYPT

ARABI

Nile

Red Sea

—— Boundary of Alexander's Empire

⟶ Alexander's campaigns

0   5   10 miles
0   5   10   15 km
Carta, Jerusalem

or important world, was left by his death not leaderless, but with too many diverse and divergent leaders. His top generals fought and schemed against each other in an enormous division of spoils. For a century, beginning about 300 B.C.E., the present region of Israel—known then as Yehud or Judea—was ruled by the Egypt-based dynasty founded by Alexander's general Ptolemy. Meanwhile, more than once efforts were made to take it by the Syria-based dynasty established by another general, Seleucus.

Finally, about 200 B.C.E., the reigning Seleucid monarch, Antiochus III, did gain control of Judea. He made and observed a pledge that, like the Ptolemaic rulers before him, he would allow his Jewish subjects to maintain their traditional rituals and religious worship unhindered. However, in the endless cycle of imperial ups and downs, new pressures came to be applied to the Seleucids from farther west—from the city-state of Rome in the slender peninsula of Italy.

The Romans had already shattered the power of Macedonia, homeland of Alexander. They then pushed Antiochus completely out of Greece and from all Asia Minor. The Seleucid monarch was desperate for more funds and for dedicated supporters to defend his remaining realm against the inexorable advances of the Roman legions.

His successors, Seleucus IV and Antiochus IV Epiphanes, continued to plot and connive, often with the high priests of the Jerusalem Temple or their jealous subordinates. These intrigues, treacherous and often bloody, had as one main object the seizing of more revenue from the Temple, to whose upkeep all male Jews were required to contribute each year.

Another aim, closely related, was the effort to hellenize the people of Judea—even to the extent of persuading them to worship the Greek Olympian gods, a numerous and somewhat unsavory assortment. Many wealthy and aristocratic Jews were already highly hellenized in their manner of living and thinking, and they saw little reason for their compatriots' stubborn resistance against the wishes of the ruler at the capital, Antioch, Syria.

The allure of Greek-style games, amusements, pleasures, and vices attracted even many of the younger priests, as well as the

[73]

merchant and financial circles in the principal towns of Judea. Hellenism was, after all, an urban and citified way of life and culture. Only peasants and "squares" hated hellenism—or so it appeared to the assimilated hellenists among the people of Israel.

The Temple and its high priesthood became a pawn in the hands of Antiochus Epiphanes. In rapid succession he unseated a series of high priests, always in favor of one who promised to get him a larger share of the Temple's substantial treasury. Finally came the appointment of particularly corrupt and incompetent hellenized priests who were not even of the Oniad branch of the Zadokite family from which high priests had traditionally been drawn since about the time of Solomon himself.

Resentment and resistance increased among the masses of Jews in Jerusalem and the countryside. This led to the placing of Syrian mercenary soldiers in fortifications commanding the Temple itself. Further resistance led to punitive massacres of Jews in Jerusalem, and finally to a series of crushing decrees in which Epiphanes tried to ban Jewish worship, diet (kosher), circumcision, and other sacred traditions. The Temple was entered, its high altar was surmounted by another shrine on which offerings were made to Olympian Zeus (Jupiter), and all the Jews in the Seleucid realm were ordered thenceforward to make sacrifices to the Olympian gods and, more or less incidentally, to honor the divine monarch Epiphanes himself. Dire punishment faced all who might refuse or resist.

The spark of resistance that finally became the flame of revolt was not struck in relatively sophisticated and luxurious Jerusalem, or even within Judea itself. In the small village of Modi'in, just outside Judea, an agent of the "divine" ruler Epiphanes arrived to make certain that pagan sacrifices were performed as required. The local Jewish priest, Mattathias of the Hasmonean family, refused to take part, and when another Jew stepped forward to do what was asked, Mattathias killed him and the imperial agent too. The militant priest with his five sons then fled and found refuge in mountainous terrain nearby.

They issued appeals for supporters, and around them gathered guerrilla groups who came to be called the Pious Ones, or *Hasidim*. (This is not to be confused with the Jewish movement that arose in Europe in the eighteenth century.) They drew their strength from the villages and the peasantry and began effective raids against the royal centers and against the collaborating Jews. The high-placed hellenizers were indignant, then alarmed. From Samaria to the north, the Seleucid governor himself led a troop of mercenaries to eradicate these rebels. Mattathias had died in the meantime, and his son Judas led the resistors, who in a sudden savage skirmish scattered the Seleucid soldiers. Judas took the governor's sword for his own in a symbolic gesture.

It was not a sword but a hammer that became identified with Judas, a hero to most Jews ever since. So swift, sharp, and shattering were the blows struck by the guerrillas under his command that he became known as "the Hammerer"—that is, Judas *Maccabeus*. Since then, he, his brothers, and the rulers who descended from them are called the Maccabeans almost as often as the Hasmoneans, their real family name.

The Hasidim hammered their way through one surprise attack after another during 165 and 164 B.C.E. They knew the country and the countryfolk well; they were part of it and them. One Seleucid commander after another suffered humiliation or worse in the effort to bring Judas and his men to justice or to leave their bodies dead in some cleft or canyon. Each new evasion or victory by the Hasidim was like a message of hope and a recruiting slogan throughout the land. Their numbers grew despite the dangers.

It was in the Hebrew month of *Kislev* that they finally hammered out a clear path up to Jerusalem itself. Seleucid mercenaries were still holed up in the Acra fortress that overlooked the Temple, but they could only watch as Judas and his Hasidim jubilantly entered that desecrated sanctuary, cleared away the shrine to Zeus, cleansed its Holy of Holies, and once again lit the lights in the great seven-branched candlestick or Menorah. Ever since, the twenty-first of Kislev has been celebrated by observing Jews as *Hanukkah*—the festival of lights.

It was not all clear sailing after that. The recovery of the Temple and restoration of its rituals were really the start rather than

[75]

the finish to the reconquest of all Judea. A long and often tangled series of campaigns, victories, partial failures, and seeming full defeats followed. Judas was a master at delay, and at hiding when necessary. Repeatedly he and his men disappeared and survived to hammer away again. His youngest brother Eleazar was killed in action, and Judas himself died fighting some ten miles north of Jerusalem in 161 B.C.E.

His place was taken by another able brother, Jonathan. He too was forced to hide, biding his time and building his forces in the Judean wilderness, traditional hideaway for rebels and outlaws. By 155 B.C.E. he had shown strength sufficient to win a treaty of a sort from the Seleucid rulers, who were being tormented by internal rivalries and troubled by resistance in other parts of their realm also. By 152 B.C.E., Jonathan seems to have cleared the final hurdle. He was administering the entire land from Jerusalem, and he had assumed the highest title possible other than king itself: high priest of the Temple.

In 147 B.C.E. a new Seleucid ruler, Demetrius II, tried to punish rebellious Judea, but the Jewish forces under Jonathan and his brother Simon showed that they had become indeed the most formidable military power in that part of the world. They went on to extend the boundaries of Maccabean rule.

A staggering setback seemed certain when Tryphon, a Seleucid regent, tricked and treacherously captured Jonathan near the site of modern Acre. Tryphon then marched his forces south and sought to swing into Jerusalem from the southwest side. The almost incredible occurrence of a snowstorm in the Judean wilderness saved the city, however.

It was the Hasmonean brother Simon who now stepped into a triple role: high priest in the Temple, highest commander of the military, and civil head of the land. Simon was the last of the living sons of Mattathias. Not even he died a natural death. A treacherous son-in-law assassinated him and his two sons. Only one son of Simon remained alive, John Hyrcanus, who assumed the high priesthood and the military-civil headship of the land.

At first Hyrcanus suffered losses and endured a siege from the forces of the Seleucid monarch, Antiochus VII Sidetes, but in 129 B.C.E. the latter was killed while fighting elsewhere in his troubled empire. During the following period of confusion and chaos, John Hyrcanus was able to recoup his losses and even to make additional gains in territory as well as in power. Once again as in the heydays of David and Solomon, the weakness of the nations beyond the borders of Israel permitted it to be ruled by its own monarchs. They ruled not always wisely, gently, or well. But there were no alien idols or altars before which Jews were expected to bow down; and there was no tribute to be taken to a court beyond the confines of their own "promised land."

The era of John Hyrcanus, lasting to 104 B.C.E., was one of expansion of boundaries and of generally rising prosperity within them. His successor, Aristobolus, though in office only the year 104–103 B.C.E., nevertheless added to the Jewish state the region of the Galilee, which was later to become especially important to the Christian religion.

There followed Alexander Yannai or Janeus, brother of Aristobolus. During more than a quarter century, ending in 76 B.C.E., in a long and costly series of wars, Yannai expanded further the area of his control, and at the same time intensified very nearly to the breaking point the resistance of a large number of his subjects against his imperious and warlike policies.

The situation that had developed within the land seems indeed more significant to us today than do all the military campaigns and sieges. As the Maccabean or Hasmonean heads of state took for themselves ever greater powers, important policy groupings, or "parties," developed among their subjects. This polarization of his people proceeded more rapidly when Yannai began to call himself king as well as high priest.

One important group included in particular the wealthiest aristocrats, courtiers, and military men in the realm. They supported the monarch, his wars of expansion, and his claims to both the high priesthood and the crown, and they insisted that the Temple and its priestly staff control all aspects of the national cult and its rituals of sacrifice. This group or party were called the

Sadducees. In their general attitudes they resembled in many ways the "hellenizers" against whom Mattathias and his sons had led their historic resistance movement.

Different in social background and policies was a less highly placed group known as the *Pharisees,* from a Hebrew word meaning those set apart or separated. Though often misunderstood by historians, the Pharisees seem in many ways linked with the attitudes of the Hasidim or pious, personally committed religionists who had resisted hellenization and fought for the right to worship in the way of their fathers.

In the era of the oppressive King Alexander Yannai, the Pharisees stressed the oral religious law, the tradition, and the popular roots of religion that reached back beyond Solomon's Temple or even David's tabernacle. They did not want to be dictated to or dominated by an arbitrary high priest. Though they accepted the Temple and the priesthood as institutions, they were disturbed that the offices of high priest and king had been assumed by the same individual. To them the monarch was a person, not a divinity, and they accorded to each pious Jew a certain individual authority and conscience which he should not have to surrender to either a high priest or a king. Further, the Pharisees approved of the local and community teachers or learned scholars of the law who came to be called *rabbis* or masters.

Much that evolved in this early Pharisee philosophy became an integral part of Judaism in the centuries of scattering and wandering that followed for most Jews.

The Pharisees were not the only ones who questioned the claims of the Maccabean kings. There were far more extreme groups, called *Essenes,* who asserted that the Maccabean-Hasmonean rulers, not being of the families from which the high priests had traditionally come, were entirely unfit to head the rituals and policies of the Temple. The Temple of Jerusalem, the Essenes insisted, had become false or tainted. They disagreed with its calendar and with many of its practices. Groups of Essenes went to live in monastic communities in the wilderness in order to show their disapproval of the way things were going in their country.

Conflict arose too because of the absolute manner in which the

[78]

king-priest tried to rule. He did not make use of the *heber* or Council of Elders who traditionally had advised the kings and had laid before them at least some of the most urgent wants of their subjects.

The bitterness finally burst out in open revolt against King Yannai. At intervals during half a decade or more, 94 to 88 B.C.E., uprisings seriously threatened his power. Pharisee leaders even called in a Seleucid monarch—a non-Jew—to aid them, and possibly someday to rule them. These combined forces defeated those of King Yannai in a battle at historic Shechem. The rebels, however, could not quite stomach another Seleucid ruler and decided against discarding their Hasmonean head. The king, for his part, seems to have learned something, for he is said to have advised his queen to keep on good terms with the Pharisees, while he again went off to his incessant wars on the boundaries of his land. He died in 76 B.C.E. while commanding a siege in the region east of the Jordan River.

His widow, Queen Alexandra Salome, did maintain peace and gave support to popular education and welfare during her reign, which ended, unfortunately, at her death in 67 B.C.E. It had been but a brief period of hope. Afterwards the land was torn by fierce and fatal struggles for royal power.

6

ISRAEL REVOLTS
AGAINST ROME

(TO ABOUT 73 C.E.)

Proclaim liberty throughout the land,
unto all the inhabitants thereof.

—LEVITICUS 25:10

Hyrcanus II, eldest son of the dead queen, was to become the next king and high priest. He too preferred peace and favored the Pharisee policies. However, his younger brother Aristobolus, a firebrand, was determined to seize the throne for himself and led an armed uprising supported by influential Sadducees and army officers. A series of complex, shameful, and almost suicidal maneuvers and intrigues followed. Both brothers tried to win by getting military help from rulers outside the land. A particular prize in their struggles, because of the combined kingly and high-priestly claims of both, was physical possession of the famous ancient Temple on Mount Moriah. With it went control of its substantial treasury supported by the entire male population of the country, and also control of its daily rituals of sacrifice.

This internal struggle was bound to attract the attention of the most ruthless and dominant of all the powers in the world at that time—Rome itself. Indeed, Roman legions under a famous commander, Pompey, were already in Syria, to take over what had been the heart of the once-mighty Seleucid empire.

By 63 B.C.E., Pompey had marched his men to Jerusalem, where the gates were opened to him by the pro-Hyrcanus faction. Their foes, the forces of Aristobolus, were occupying the Temple itself atop Mount Moriah. The Romans besieged it, and when it was finally captured, Pompey strode into the sacred building searching for its secrets. His gentile feet desecrated its holy places, but he neither plundered nor destroyed this unique shrine of Jewish worship.

The land we call Israel was trapped in the net of Roman power and greed. Efforts were made to break free of Rome in 57 B.C.E., but they failed. From then on, every major intrigue or power struggle within Rome itself was reflected in intrigues and power struggles in Israel, which the Romans named *Judea*.

Rome was undergoing bloody changes, completing the transformation of the onetime republic into an absolute and arbitrary imperial rule, under which it was for a time to shine and then, during a long and harrowing finale, to decline. Pompey was eliminated by Julius Caesar; then Caesar himself was assassinated. In the following struggles, Judea, like nearby Egypt, became part of the empire ruled by the "playboy" politician Mark Antony. He, like Caesar before him, became the lover of Cleopatra, the Ptolemaic dynasty princess who had taken over the throne of the pharaohs. For a brief interval a Maccabean prince, Antigonous, claimed both the kingship and the high priest's position in Judea, but he was captured by the Romans and beheaded.

Amid intrigues and battles that led to the defeat and death of Mark Antony and Cleopatra and to the triumph of Caesar's nephew Augustus, first of the Roman emperors, one of the most gifted yet despicable careerists in history was climbing toward power in Judea. His name was Herod. He was the son of a relatively minor official from the southern land of Idumea, which had been conquered and converted to Judaism by King Alexander Yannai.

Pious Jews could not look on Herod as a genuine member of the house of Israel. Herod himself posed as a pious Jew when convenient to his career, but acted more Roman than the Romans when to do so would best serve his aims.

By 37 B.C.E., Herod had maneuvered and crawled to a point where he could claim kingship in Judea with Roman approval. He could not, of course, assume also the influential position of high priest, but he was adept at manipulating and dominating the many contenders for that post. During a decade or more Herod showed an almost unbelievable talent for survival, while he slowly strengthened his control in Judea, often by the cruelest of means.

He proved a good gatherer of taxes and tribute for Rome. No matter who rose to the top of the heap in Rome, Herod became that person's supporter and agent. He flattered, bribed, praised, and did dirty jobs for the increasingly corrupt Roman establishment. In short, he was enormously useful to the elite of that empire.

By 24 B.C.E., Herod was firmly in the saddle and pulling hard on the reins that guided the people of Judea. He was not a stupid man, though a sadistic and oftentimes psychotic one. His psychoses, however, were not the sort that made him less able to sense and adjust to the changing political winds.

Herod's constant need to win acceptance and esteem from his subjects, who generally despised or hated him, led him into a series of large and costly building projects. The most famous and important of these, begun about 23 B.C.E., was a new and more beautiful Temple for Jerusalem. It was built where the old ones had stood, and in such a way as not to interrupt the routines of ritual and sacrifice. Hence it is often called "the second Temple," just as is the earlier more modest one built under Zerub-babel after the return from Babylon.

Built of white marble and gold, a structure of commanding splendor, it became known, as he hoped it would, as "Herod's Temple." Though not a large building by modern standards, it was an exquisite one, and it surmounted a huge platform, contained by stone walls whose enormous blocks still impress visitors to its last remnant—the Western Wall in modern Jerusalem.

Construction of the Temple required many years. By the year 5 B.C.E., however, the new Temple of Herod was already in use and had become the goal of pilgrimages by Jews who lived outside as well as those within Judea itself.

In the winter of that year, 5 B.C.E., a son was born to a Jewish mother, Mary, and her husband, Joseph, a poor carpenter, in the tiny Galilean village of Nazareth. These devout Jews, among the humblest of Herod's many subjects, gave their firstborn the good Jewish name of Joshua, or Jeshua, later called Jesus.

An elaborate tradition and theology has accumulated around

[85]

the figure of this popular Jewish teacher, preacher, moralist, and agitator. His actual birth was later said to have occurred in Bethlehem, where his parents had gone to register for a census that was to be taken for tax purposes. In that way the birth of the humble carpenter Jesus was linked with the native city of King David rather than with the less impressive Nazareth.

Four different narratives, or gospels, of his life and teachings were written, all long after his death. Attributed to Matthew, Mark, Luke, and John, they form the first books of the new or Christian Bible. They include two different father-to-son lists or genealogies to prove that Jesus, through his earthly father Joseph, was a direct descendant of the great kings David and Solomon. One such list, given in the gospel of Matthew, extends all the way from Father Abraham to Jesus, with three groups of fourteen ancestors each, perhaps because the Hebrew letters for DVD (David) mean also the number 14! (D stood for 4, V for 6; $D + V + D = 14$.)

It might seem odd that this unassuming teacher and preacher, whose chosen disciples, companions, and audiences were people as humble as himself, should be linked to the royal past of Israel, and even to the splendid monarch Solomon! But it is more easily understood in the light of the great hope or longing for a Messiah that had come alive in the masses of the people in those bitter days of Roman domination.

Roman rule, callous and corrupt when not actually vicious, generated resentment among the Judeans. Their religion and their past experiences unsuited them to remain subservient to an alien rule for long. Was not this still their own "promised land"? The Lord had not led them from Egyptian bondage to make them serfs of this pagan empire extending over the world from Italy. Some of their parents or grandparents had resisted the oppressive rule of King Alexander Yannai, one of their own co-religionists. How, then, could they remain quiet under the iron heel of the corrupt Roman rule?

Various factions developed, beginning with the years when Herod was king. An influential but rather small group of the wealthy formed the "Herodians," for they supported him, partly because he so clearly had the power, partly because of his manifest ability to get along with the head men in Rome no matter how things changed there. The Herodian position was to avoid giving serious offense either to Roman wishes or to Jewish sensibilities. Jews were, in fact, exempted from Roman military service; Roman images were not forced on Jews to worship; and the Roman legionnaires who occupied the land were told not to interfere with ordinary Jewish religious rituals or gatherings.

The former Sadducees, the party that had closely supported the Maccabean rulers in the past, were now disunited. Some were concerned mainly with upholding the influence and prestige of the glorious Jerusalem Temple under its current high priest. Others were determined that somehow an independent all-Jewish state, such as they had before under the Maccabean rulers, be restored.

This demand for a return to self-rule was most active in an extreme group called the *Zealots*. They insisted that the only way to regain the freedoms that made life worthwhile was to fight for them even though it meant openly defying the might of Rome. The Zealot creed called for recognition of no emperor, Roman or otherwise, and of no other monarch. Their burning slogan "No king but God himself!" gained many adherents.

However, the group with the greatest influence among the masses of common people came to be the Pharisees, already mentioned. Their leaders at first interpreted the hateful rule of Rome as God's punishment for the mistakes and misdeeds of the people of Israel. Hence the Roman yoke should be borne with patience, while utmost attention should be given by every man to the religious laws and to sincere worship, in the hope that God would relent and forgive.

Feared by almost all, even by his followers, and hated bitterly by many, Herod died at last in 4 B.C.E. It was his wish that Jerusalem and most of Judea be ruled by his son Archelaus, no less cruel and capricious than Herod, but far less shrewd and able.

During the Passover festival of 3 B.C.E., protest demonstrations against Archelaus and Roman rule took place in Jerusalem. Archelaus sent in soldiers who killed thousands of demonstrators. Then he ordered all pilgrims to leave the city. The Roman governor of Syria arrived soon with troops to crush the uprisings, now spreading throughout Judea. Archelaus, who had received from Rome only the title of *ethnarch*, not king, lasted a mere nine years. So many protests against him were carried to Rome that he was sent off to Gaul in 6 c.e. (Christian or Common Era).

Now began the direct rule—or misrule—of Judea by *procurators*, a low grade of governor or administrator sent out from Rome. They set up their headquarters in Caesarea, collected taxes directly through various agents, and enriched themselves as rapidly as they could by many kinds of graft and fraud. Appointment of procurators was generally a matter of buying the position, which went most often to greedy men who paid well for the license to go to a distant region and grow rich at the expense of its population. They generally regarded the Jews as barbaric or inferior, stayed only until they had made their "pile," and then returned to the decadent comforts and pleasures of the imperial city that ruled the world. Even the best of the procurators proved unwelcome to most Judeans. The worst seemed utterly intolerable—far worse, in fact, than Herod.

The everyday world was so disturbing to most of the common people that they took refuge in dreams of a brighter, better future. Obviously, relief could not come from Rome or from the well-fed officials of the Temple, or even from the seventy-one members of the great council, or *Sanhedrin*, which dealt with Jewish affairs under the watchful eyes of the Roman procurators.

How then could the better world come about? It would have to come from God, who would initiate it by sending to earth a redeemer or *Messiah*, the Hebrew word for "The Anointed One," meaning a divinely chosen king. Thus arose and flourished the intoxicating vision of the Messiah, the Greek for which, *Christos*, became attached later to the name of the Galilean carpenter-teacher-reformer, Jesus (the) Christ, meaning Jeshua the Messiah.

Jesus traveled in the land for about two years, accompanied by his disciples, who shared everything in common. He sought out the poor, the humble, the despised, the sick, the rejected. He taught by means of radiant, often cryptic, parables and figures of speech. His message was one of utter love and forgiveness from man to man, in preparation for that awaited new world, the Kingdom of God on earth. He did not call for violent resistance to the Romans, as did the Zealots. Many of his words were in keeping rather with the views of the pacifist Pharisees. Thus, when a questioner sought to trip him up by asking whether Jews ought to pay taxes to Rome, Jesus evaded the trap. Calling attention to the emperor's image on a coin, he replied, "Give to Caesar that which is Caesar's and to God that which is God's."

He was capable also of indignation and even of physical protest, as when he lashed the money-changers and merchants out of the courts of the sacred Temple in Jerusalem. At every stage he accepted and observed the established Jewish law, but he tried to touch the spirit within it, not merely the husk of words in which it was wrapped.

Then came the springtime, at the Passover, when Jesus made a triumphal entrance into Jerusalem, acclaimed by the common people. He was soon seized as a troublemaker. According to the books of the Christian Bible, leading figures in the Sanhedrin, dedicated to collaboration with the Romans, feared that his influence would bring disaster. He was sentenced by the Roman procurator of that time, Pontius Pilate, to be executed by the savage Roman method of crucifixion. Thus, shortly after the Passover, in 30 or 31 C.E., Jesus died on Golgotha, the hill of skulls, outside Jerusalem's walls. But neither his influence nor the evils against which he preached came to an end with his death.

Caligula became Roman emperor in 37 C.E. and insanely tried to have his statue set up for worship within the Temple at Jerusalem. Rabid Zealots and the less extreme Pharisees alike protested against this as an outrageous impiety. Under the next emperor, Claudius, the series of unpopular procurators was interrupted for a time by a less objectionable ruler of Judea: Agrippa I, grandson of Herod and of the Jewish Hasmonean princess Mariamne whom Herod had married on his way up the ladder of power.

After Agrippa's death, the sequence of corrupt, stupid, or brutalized procurators was resumed. By 66 C.E. a new low was reached when a rascal named Florus held that important office and the notorious Nero was emperor in Rome. Conditions in Judea had now reached the breaking point. Finally, leading Pharisees chose, perhaps reluctantly, to call for open resistance to Rome— the course so long urged by the Zealots. (Many Pharisees, however, including the famous rabbi Yohanan ben Zakai, still urged a policy of nonviolence and nonresistance.)

The first spark burst into flame at Caesarea. A civil rights struggle there between Jews and non-Jewish residents led to violence and the flight of the Jews from the city. Still more massive protest actions followed in Jerusalem, where many Jews were gathered for the traditional harvest festival of *Succoth*. Zealot militants under Menahem overwhelmed the Roman garrison at Herod's old southern hideaway of Masada on a mount overlooking the Dead Sea. Then, with Masada in their hands, they moved north to Jerusalem and overcame the Roman soldiers holding that city.

In the Temple the priests, though traditionally Sadducees and aristocrats, refused to make the customary sacrifices in honor of the pagan emperor in Rome. It was a symbolic declaration of independence by the Jews.

The forces under Florus could not cope with the revolt, now spreading like wildfire. Cestius Gallus, governor of Syria and top Roman official in all the region, marched his legionnaires southward in a deadly procession, destroying towns and devastating whole districts. It was planned that Jerusalem suffer the same punishment, but there the resistance proved so fierce that the Romans were forced to pull back. They were badly beaten at the pass of Beth-Horon.

The rift with Rome was now complete. But Jewish forces were tragically divided in leadership and aims. Menahem, the brilliant Zealot militant, was assassinated by Sadducees who feared he would further arouse Rome to vengeance. Emergency steps were taken to defend the country against the inevitable new blows from the world's greatest military power.

Those blows began when Vespasian, ablest of Rome's commanders, arrived at the head of veteran legions and began a bloody advance, taking the Galilee and then one after another of the key towns and strong points of Judea. By mid-69 C.E. the Roman juggernaut had overrun all but Jerusalem and a triangular segment of territory that took in the Masada hilltop fortress, still held by Zealots.

By early 70 C.E. Vespasian had returned to Rome, where he became emperor largely through the strong support of army legions. His son Titus, left behind to finish the job in Judea, proceeded with relentless thoroughness, though not without unexpected difficulties and delays. His armies besieged Jerusalem in a long, bitter, and heartbreaking action. A former Jewish commander named Josephus, who had gone over to the Romans, shouted invitations to his former companions in arms to surrender without further resistance. Later, safe in Rome, Josephus wrote a famous history of the war and also a history of the Jewish people.

Starvation decimated the population locked within Jerusalem's walls. Nevertheless, and despite internal disagreements that continued even then, they held out against the most feared military machine in the ancient world.

In August of 70 C.E.—the ninth day of the month of *Av* in the Jewish calendar—the Romans finally broke through. They took the Temple amid ferocious fires and heavy bloodshed. Then the Temple and all of Jerusalem were systematically plundered and afterwards even more systematically destroyed. A terrible example was being made in the effort to show all other subject peoples of Rome that rebellion was costly and hopeless.

Among the few surviving remnants of the great Jerusalem before that destruction is a part of the western retaining wall erected during Herod's rule to secure the base on which the Temple rested. Sometimes called "the Wailing Wall" but properly known as "the Western Wall," it has become an outdoor synagogue for Jewish worship and is visited annually by thousands of Israelis and travelers from near and far.

[91]

Titus marched off thousands of Jewish captives from Jerusalem and elsewhere in the conquered land. They were used as the victims in gladiatorial games and as slave labor in Rome. About 700 of them survived to reach Rome itself. There Titus, his father the emperor, and his brother Domitian shared in a traditional triumphal procession. Sacred objects taken from the Temple, including its famous great seven-branched candelabra or Menorah, were carried along as trophies. It was a kind of Roman carnival to celebrate the "final" crushing of Judea and the punishment of its insolent, seditious Jews who had bitten the Roman hand that held their leash.

One surviving Jewish resistance leader was not dragged along the streets of Rome as a captive: Eleazar ben Yair, nephew of Menahem. With his Zealot forces and their families Eleazar had escaped to the Masada fortress. There they continued to hold out month after month, year after year. Finally, after building a complete system of encircling camps and barriers around its base and a huge cumbersome ramp to its summit, the Romans dared at last to storm the summit of Masada. They chose the time of the Passover of 73 C.E. When they entered this dearly bought citadel they found every one of its 960 defenders dead; only two women and a few children remained alive. With Roman victory inevitable, the defenders had died in a mutual suicide pact rather than be killed or enslaved by their conquerors.

The revolt of the Jews of Judea deeply shook the superpower of Rome. The revolt had gone further and held out far longer than could have been expected. It was a kind of "moral victory" but at a terrible cost for the people of what became today's Israel. In their last extremity, as the Roman legions began to crush them, they had looked for, hoped for, dreamed of massive aid from large and in some cases prosperous communities of Jews living far beyond the borders of the "promised land." Such help did not then arrive to any important extent, even from communities not totally under the yoke of Rome. This too became a lesson for the future of the Jewish spirit of resistance, which somehow was never eradicated. Rome had taken almost seven desperate years to wipe out the last of the "First Revolt" of Judea. Goliath had defeated David this time. Jerusalem lay in ruins. But Rome had lost manpower and prestige in the process. The Roman imperial government issued boasts and minted coins proclaiming that Judea now lay vanquished, broken, captive. The glorious and world-famous Temple, symbol till then of Judaism as a religion and cult, was no more. Yet—as some of the more perceptive Roman leaders soon suspected—the descendants of Jacob, who had dared wrestle with God and man, were not cured of their willingness to face enormous, even overwhelming, odds in their efforts to win liberty.

7

BAR KOCHBA, RISING STAR OF ISRAEL

(TO ABOUT 135)

"God, you needn't bother to help us—
just don't help our enemies!"

> —reputed prayer of Bar Kochba,
> leader of the Second Jewish Revolt
> against Rome.

The deliberate destruction of Jerusalem and its great Temple proved shattering to many of the Jews who survived in Judea. It was especially demoralizing to the wealthy and aristocratic, including families who had supplied priests and high officials under Herod. Many went over to the Roman upper classes, seeking to merge themselves with the pagan conquerors. Most, however, clung to their faith and the land that had fostered it.

In spite of widespread devastation of Jewish towns and villages —in Judea, in the Galilee to the north, and in Idumea to the south —a great many Jewish settlements managed to survive. The Roman rulers, firmly in control again, found it impossible to make their own armies of occupation do the work of the farms and estates they had taken over from former Jewish owners. And those armies had to be fed. Hence the Romans used Jews to work the land as peasants or tenant serfs. Even some minor administrative jobs had to be filled by Jews.

Before the defeat of the Jewish revolt, religious and political questions of importance had been settled for the Jews by the high council or *Sanhedrin* in Jerusalem. Now with Jerusalem and the Temple destroyed, a great vacuum existed.

It was filled in part by the efforts of Yohanan ben Zakai, a pacifist Pharisee. The Romans, through their spies, knew and approved of his stand against continuing resistance to Rome. During the Roman siege he had been smuggled out of Jerusalem, had met Vespasian, and had received permission to set up a religious school at Jabneh. Jewish scholars and teachers gathered there, and after Jerusalem fell, ben Zakai converted the Sanhedrin into a kind of teachers' council called the *Bet Din*. It came to rule the remaining Jewish settlements as the final authority in all intra-Jewish matters. Thus at least some aspects of Jewish life began to function again in a unified manner.

Now seeking to rule Judea directly, the Romans dealt with the president of the revived Sanhedrin, using him as the representative of surviving Jews in all matters of importance to Rome. This grew to be a hereditary post of spiritual leadership. Its occupant was called the *patriarch*. A series of rabbis, addressed as *Nasi* or prince, served as patriarchs. They claimed descent through the great Rabbi Hillel from King David.

A small Jewish group managed to stay in Jerusalem, mainly around the encampment of the Tenth Roman Legion. Thus a few Jews resided in their former capital, side by side with the Judeo-Christians and the Roman soldiers. Some records tell of seven synagogues in Jerusalem during this period, though it is not clear whether all were used at once.

The Jabneh school and the Bet Din acted like spiritual cement, holding together Jewish traditions and building further upon them. In this period of seeming subjugation the present Bible was assembled, including Ecclesiastes and the Song of Songs, but leaving for the so-called Apocrypha many books whose value was regarded as doubtful.

Sacrifices and worship could no longer be conducted at a Temple, but prayer elsewhere was declared to be equally effective. Religious services for small groups or congregations were developed. Thus the former monopoly of the central Temple gave way to more independent and numerous local synagogues.

The Jewish Revolt, though bloodily crushed, had made Judea even more important in Roman eyes. It had taken some three to four legions to subdue these obstinate people. Now instead of being turned over to some hack politician and grafter called a procurator, Judea was ruled by a Roman senator, generally one with judicial experience, and with more authority to make important changes than procurators had possessed.

Between the governor's site at Caesarea and the trouble spot Jerusalem, where the Tenth Legion was stationed, a new road was built. Other new Roman roads gave their soldiers easier access to outlying parts of the land.

A brief period of less severe oppression came during the rule of Emperor Nerva, lasting only sixteen months, 96–98 C.E., during which time policies of reconciliation seem to have been pursued. The next emperor, Trajan, annexed the Kingdom of Nabatea and thus created the Roman province of *Arabia*, east of the Jordan valley. A good new road, the *Via Nova*, was built from Damascus in the north through this Arabian province south to Eilat. It provided another means of travel in addition to the coastal road and the existing road through the Negev. Caravan trade increased, bringing greater prosperity to Arabia, somewhat at the cost of Judea.

These periods of relative quiet proved merely temporary. Trajan increasingly was concerned with war against the Parthians, who occupied much of what is now Iran. While he was thus engaged, the Jews once again rose against their Roman overlords —this time in the colonies of Egypt, Libya, Cyrenaica (part of present-day Libya), and Cyprus. For three years they fought bitterly against the forces of Lucius Quietus, a Moorish prince who had distinguished himself by his cruelty toward the Jews in Babylonia and Mesopotamia. Trajan rewarded him by making him a Roman senator and governor of Judea with full powers over its inhabitants. In the meantime, Trajan's intended conquest of Parthia and the East failed.

The next emperor, Aelius Hadrian, who ruled between 117 and 138 C.E., sought to stabilize the existing empire, abandoning his predecessor's plans for further eastern conquests. But in Judea, resentment grew against the cruelties of Quietus. Historians differ regarding Hadrian's original intention toward his Judean subjects. Some have written that he promised the Jews they could rebuild their Temple if they would only give up all weapons and completely accept Roman rule. Others deny he made any such offer. But it is certain that Hadrian summoned Quietus back to

Rome and had him executed. Perhaps he did this to pacify the Jews, but more likely he saw in Quietus a threat to his own position.

Hadrian in any case assured the Roman Senate that there was nothing further to fear from the Jews in Judea. Coins were minted showing Hadrian, clad in toga, raising a kneeling Jew, while he received the tribute of palm branches from three boys, probably symbolizing Judea, Samaria, and Galilee, all Jewish-inhabited provinces.

In 130 C.E. Hadrian visited Jerusalem and decided to rebuild it as a Roman colonial city, to be called *Colonia Aelia Capitolina* in honor of himself and of the chief pagan gods, Jupiter, Juno, and Minerva—the "Capitoline Trio." A temple to Jupiter was to rise where the Jewish Temples of Solomon and Herod had once stood. Tinaeus Rufus, then Roman governor in Judea, dedicated the site, laying out the new boundaries with a plow in the traditional Roman fashion. The plow furrows cut across the old Temple foundations.

Coins were minted to glorify the city-to-be. Hadrian had already issued an edict against "mutilation," which banned also the Jewish requirement of circumcision. Plans for the pagan shrine on their hallowed site added to the anger of the surviving Jews in Judea.

Two generations had gone by since the crushing of their first great revolt against Rome. Their respected leader was now the eminent scholar and teacher, Rabbi Akiba ben Joseph, a former shepherd whose many gifts had raised him to heights of prestige. He was able to persuade most of the members of the Sanhedrin to sanction a new revolt. Plans were made carefully, in the effort to avoid old mistakes. The Jews assigned by the Romans to manufacture weapons purposely made many slightly defective. These, when rejected and returned for replacement, were repaired by the Jewish workers, then hidden in caves and tunnels in the Judean mountains. Camouflaged forts were erected in open country in order to avoid entrapment. Akiba himself traveled widely inside and outside the Roman empire, collecting funds and aid for the planned revolt.

The chosen commander was Simon bar Kosiba, better known

as Bar Kochba, the Aramaic name which Akiba gave him, meaning "Son of the Star." His great strength, his fierceness, and his personal magnetism engendered many legends of his superhuman valor. Akiba even hailed him as the Messiah come at last. "Kosiba has risen as a star (*kochba*) in Jacob," he said. Bar Kochba was said to have been a descendant of David and of the Hasmonean-Maccabean heroes.

In the legends recounted by his enemies and friends he was said to have demanded extreme courage of his men. One story relates that he required them to submit to the amputation of one finger to prove their bravery. He raised an army of about 400,000 and is reported to have told the Lord confidently: "God, you needn't bother to help us—just don't help our enemies!"

Bar Kochba's boldness unified and inspired his followers. Even Samaritans and gentiles joined his forces, eager to escape the yoke of Rome.

At the end of the harvest season in 132 C.E. the planned revolt erupted some twenty miles northwest of Jerusalem, near the site of the present great Israeli airport of Lydda (Lod).

To guard against possible Jewish outbreaks, the Romans had stationed near Jerusalem in 131 C.E. their formidable Sixth Legion, "Ironsides." Even so, they were staggered by the power and fury of this new Jewish revolt. The Tenth Legion and the non-Jewish residents had to be evacuated from Jerusalem to Caesarea. Once again the city of David and the Temple were ruled by Jews.

Recent finds by archeologists in the Judean desert indicate that Bar Kochba guided a complete and efficient administration. Akiba was head of the Sanhedrin. Coinage, taxation, military organization, and legal matters all were handled by the new Jewish government. Bar Kochba was known by the title of Simeon, Prince of Israel. Sacrifices were resumed at the remnants of the Temple in Jerusalem. The calendar was dated to begin with the revolt, so that 132 C.E. became Year One of the Redemption of Israel. As late as Year Four the regime was still operating. In their religious zeal, Bar Kochba's soldiers defaced Roman bronze vessels to remove likenesses of human figures, then forbidden by Jewish religious law.

Bar Kochba's astounding successes in Judea led him to seek to penetrate the Galilee also. It seems that the majority of Jews there did not, however, join him. Yet he gained control of part of Samaria. His supporters included some oppressed Christians from the lower classes of the Roman empire. However, the Judeo-Christians, born Jews converted to Christianity, having newly recognized Jesus as the Messiah, could not accept Bar Kochba in that role and refused to serve in his forces. They were severely persecuted by the rebels. This widened the gap between Jews and Christians who had been born as Jews.

Rome, with its boundaries already shrinking elsewhere, was sorely stricken by this large-scale revolt. Hadrian had to recall his best general, Julius Severus, from the task of subduing a Celt revolt in Britain. To Severus's army were added picked fighters from all parts of the still vast Roman empire, until the count came finally to 100,000 men. They moved carefully, warned by the example of the Twenty-Second Roman Legion which had rushed directly into the Judean countryside and had been wiped out by the rebels.

Again a ponderous Roman military juggernaut consumed the country, surrounding, capturing, killing, and burning everything Jewish in its path. More than 950 villages and towns, fifty forti-fied places, and hundreds of thousands of Jewish rebels fell into Roman hands. Only when Jerusalem was retaken and converted again into the pagan city of Aelia Capitolina did Hadrian feel safe in returning to Rome.

In the midst of defeat, Bar Kochba and the last remnant of his men found refuge in Beit Ter some eight miles southwest of Jerusalem itself. In this makeshift fortress they held out for about a year. Only in the late summer of 135 C.E., using elaborate ramps and siege machinery, as they had done at Masada, did the Romans finally break through and overwhelm the rebels, leaving alive not one of the remaining heroes.

Legend attributes the death of Bar Kochba to a scorpion bite rather than to a Roman sword. The legend may have arisen be-cause to his followers it was unthinkable that a mere Roman could have killed their fabled leader. The tales tell, too, of the river of blood that flooded up to the bellies of the Roman horses as they entered Beit Ter—a river that bore corpses down to the sea itself. The fall of Beit Ter occurred on the ninth day of Ab, the date on which the Temple had twice before been destroyed—first by Babylonians, then by Romans in 70 C.E. Bones of Bar Kochba's men who fled to caves in the cliffs around En-gedi on the Dead Sea have been found in recent years.

Death had deeply drained the remaining manpower of Judea. During the three years of this great Second Revolt, each side seems to have suffered enormous loss of life. Rome had won, technically speaking, but had undergone a serious decline in resources and also in prestige. Hadrian did not even dare to report to the Senate the traditional victory message: "I and my army are well." The senators, however, blind in their wealth and illusion of security, ordered coins struck on which were inscribed *Exercitus Judaicus* (Thanks to the army victorious over the Jews).

Punishment of captives and survivors was fiendishly cruel. The horrors of these vengeances reflected the terror that the Romans had felt in the face of Bar Kochba and his freedom fighters. Many Jews escaped to Asia, Africa, or Parthia. Seaports were jammed with refugees. Captive Jews were sold as slaves in such numbers that prices fell in the great slave markets. Numbers were slaughtered in the Roman gladiatorial games that provided spectacles for the passive populations of the empire. As a final horror, the Romans banned the burial of Jewish corpses. The "promised land" was blighted by the sight and the stench of decaying bodies, the ultimate outrage to both living and dead. But in the midst of the terror, heroic and pious Jews managed by stealth and in the darkness to bury some of the remains. And so a tradition was born that has persisted through the years. Modern Israeli soldiers often have risked death or died under fire in their efforts to regain the bodies of their dead from battlefields.

8

THE TALMUD

(TO ABOUT 300)

We thank you, O Lord . . . for your Torah,
which you have taught us,
and for your laws,
which you have made known to us.

—FROM THE JEWISH PASSOVER SERVICE
(*The Haggadah*)

Known as Aelia Capitolina, the former Jerusalem was now garrisoned by Roman soldiers and settled by gentile Syrians and Arabs. The sole remaining trace of the Jewish Temple was the segment of Herodian wall on the western side of Mount Moriah. A temple to Venus (Aphrodite) stood just about where the present Church of the Holy Sepulchre stands. In this thoroughly pagan city were statues of Roman, Greek, and Phoenician gods, as well as statues of Hadrian and other prominent Romans.

Neither Jews nor even Judeo-Christians were permitted, under pain of death, to enter the city. In one instance even a Christian bishop, because of his Jewish background, was replaced by one of gentile birth. The Jews who were now scattered widely throughout the known world cherished the memory of the Bar Kochba revolt, keeping alive its legends as a powerful bond among them.

Hadrian tried to wipe out Judaism as a religion in Judea, for he now regarded it as a recurring source of Jewish resistance. Reading or teaching the Torah, owning a copy of it, observing the Saturday Sabbath, or practicing circumcision—all were punishable crimes. However, the Romans did not, even in this dark period, try to force their pagan worship on Jews, Judeo-Christians, or other Christians who still survived in or around the land now known as Israel.

Judea had become a "consular province" of Rome, garrisoned permanently by the Tenth and Sixth Legions. The hated and

JUDEA
CONSULAR PROVINCE OF ROME,
THEN CALLED SYRIA PALESTINE

Euphrates R.

Tarsus●

●Aleppo

Antioch●

Salamis●

CYPRUS

S Y R I A

Byblos●

Mediterranean Sea

Sidon●

●Damascus

Tyre●

Acre (Acco)●

Sea of Galilee

Caesarea●

JUDEA
SYRIA PALESTINE

Joppa● Lod●

Jabneh● Jerusalem●

Ashkelon●

Gaza●

Masada●

A R A B I A   P E T R A E A

Jordan R.

Dead Sea

N A B A T E A N S

Petra●

E G Y P T

Nile R.

Aila●

0 20 40 60 miles
0 40 80 km
Carta, Jerusalem

—————— Boundary of the Roman Empire
••••••••••••• Boundary of Provincia Judea

feared name of Judea was blotted out. Instead, the Romans called it "Syria Palestine." It was a ruined and impoverished country, containing only about 800,000 Jews, compared with about 1,500,-000 before the Bar Kochba revolt.

In Judea, the number of known Jewish villages had been reduced to forty-two from more than one hundred before the revolt. Large areas from which the Romans had expelled all Jews were now settled by Arabs and Syrians. In the Jordan Valley, however, some Jews were retained as laborers on Roman-run plantations where balsam was grown.

About half a dozen large Jewish villages remained throughout some two hundred years in southern Judea. There were still Jews in the coastal cities of Gaza and Ascalon. A little farther north, around Jabneh and Lod, the Jewish population was heavier. Still farther north, in Apollonia on the coast between Jaffa (Joppa) and Caesarea, there were some Jewish residents. Jaffa remained almost entirely Jewish.

Most of the surviving Jewish scholars managed to ride out the worst of the Roman bloodbaths by going to the Galilee district. There, some fifty-six Jewish villages still remained out of sixty-four. Immigrants reached there also from Babylonia and from Cappadocia, making the Galilee the center of Jewish studies for the entire land of Israel.

Hadrian died in 138 C.E. and was followed by Antonius Pius, who soon faced another Jewish uprising. It was suppressed by the governor of Syria Palestine. Pius later withdrew some of the harshest of the anti-Jewish decrees dating back to Hadrian. Burial of the dead soldiers' corpses was now allowed, and circumcision might again be performed, but still no Jew was permitted to enter what had been Jerusalem.

Jewish will to survive showed itself again when at the village of Usha in western Galilee were assembled the leaders who had survived in the region, and some of Akiba's followers who had found refuge in Babylon. They reviewed the revolt, the disaster of its defeat, the harsh measures that followed it, and the possibilities for Jewish survival in future. They made proposals for reviving and strengthening Jewish traditions, well aware that many Jews who had not been killed in the great struggle had subsequently been lost to the faith by conversion to Christianity, or lost to the country by emigration.

An important decision was made: a sort of Sanhedrin-like body would be revived consisting of the traditional seventy-one scholars and men learned in the religious law. The office of patriarch, or spiritual head for the Jewish people, was revived also. Simeon ben Gamaliel served in that capacity from 140 to 165 C.E.

His son Judah became the next patriarch. He possessed considerable wealth and the will to use it for the benefit of his coreligionists. Judah managed to work with the Roman authorities to gain concessions of great value, including the exemption of Jews from Roman military service and the right of Jews to maintain and use their own courts, to own property, to levy taxes, and so on. In exchange, they pledged to give up further attempts to rebel. The ban against Jews living in what had been Jerusalem was continued, but Jews were allowed to pay visits there.

Judah's great legacy includes also his labor of fifty years—codification of the *Halakah,* or Oral Law. This rich outgrowth of the Torah (the first five books of the Bible) had been handed down by word of mouth through many generations. Judah thus carried to completion the labors of many scholars before him, including the great rabbis Hillel, Akiba, and Meir. *Mishnah,* meaning "repetition," is the name of this epoch-making compilation of Jewish laws and regulations covering every aspect of life, birth, death, marriage, divorce, hygiene, agriculture, welfare, war, peace, the protection of labor, criminal and civil law, and—above all—religious worship. Interspersed with these rules are legends, folktales, and traditions.

The six tractates or divisions of the Mishnah have titles such as Seeds, Feasts, Women, Damages, Sacred Things, and Purifications. Behind this monumental compilation lay the thinking and interpretations of 148 teachers, or *Tanaim,* from the time of Hillel onward. The completion of the Mishnah early in the third century C.E. saved from extinction a rich tradition and, indeed, an entire way of life.

Learning, especially in the religious law, had long been looked on as essential for Jewish survival. Now in the third century Jewish schools were established at more than one place in what has since become Israel. Besides the famed center of Tiberias in the Galilee, there were schools also in Caesarea on the coast. These served the coastal area between there and Jaffa, called the Sharon, which retained a mixed Jewish-Samaritan population. Jewish centers of some importance were also at Haifa; at Ptolemais (now called Acre); at Achzib north of Ptolemais; and at Scythopolis, now Beth-shean, near the east bank of the Jordan.

Grief over the loss of the Temple at Jerusalem remained great, but it did not halt efforts to meet current and future needs. Emigration from the "promised land" had grown alarmingly. The rabbis discouraged it, finding relevant religious grounds to persuade Jews not to forsake their land of promise.

The needs of Jews everywhere were not overlooked. A new calendar, based on the cycles of the moon but adjusted to the sun also, was perfected. Jews had previously conversed in Aramaic or in Greek. Now the ancient and venerated Hebrew was revived as a literary language.

The hold of the land of Israel even on Jews who lived elsewhere continued to be powerful. A Jewish burial place from 200 C.E., excavated near Haifa, has been found to contain remains of Jews brought fifteen hundred miles from Arabia to be buried in Palestine, as Israel was then called. Jews from other distant places were also brought back to the sacred soil.

Roman-style cities, public buildings, and culture prevailed in the land from about 100 to 300 C.E. Each city had its Roman style marketplace, bath, theaters, aqueducts, and public buildings, ostentatious in a way that impressed Roman tastes. Some of the cities were walled; all were tied together by Roman roads. Jews took little part in Roman city life. They kept to the countryside and to their own villages, except for the two Galilean towns of Tiberias and Sepphoris.

Judaism remained a permitted religion (*religio licita*), even though emperors after Pius did not pass laws favorable to Jews. The former city of Jerusalem continued to be forbidden to Jews, and they were discouraged from converting others to their faith. Only in 212 c.e. did they receive full Roman citizenship under the Emperor Caracalla. However, by this time the Jews in the land of Israel had become a people apart rather than the main force and foundation in the life of that land.

Christians, other than Judeo-Christians, had never been banned from Jerusalem. Early in the third century c.e. began the first pilgrimages to the Jerusalem "holy places" associated with the life of the Jew known as Jesus the Christ. The first Christian church was built there on Mount Zion, David's particular hill, not far from Mount Moriah where Solomon had built his Temple. At other places in the Roman territory called Syria Palestine, Christian communities and churches began to appear. As elsewhere in the Roman empire, Christianity was gaining influence and paganism declining. That decline led to an easing of the old Jewish ban against representing the human figure in art, for the danger of idolatry seemed to be gone. Jewish synagogues and even tombstones from the fourth to the sixth century often contain reliefs or mosaics showing figures of animals or human beings.

The Roman empire whose iron heel had rested on the necks of so many of the world's peoples was now on the way down. High prices, heavy taxes, and economic crises created accelerating decay. One adventurer succeeded another as emperor. Violence and massive crime increased. Though the Jews in the land of Israel were not forced to serve as Roman soldiers, they suffered much from robbery by passing armies. The general crisis of the Roman empire hit the little land hard. The patriarchate, an inherited position, could do nothing to ease the sufferings of the Jews there, and its prestige and influence declined. However, the standing of the Sanhedrin in Syria Palestine grew, and so too did that of the great Jewish community in Babylon.

By 219 c.e. the first of two influential Jewish academies had been established in Babylon, whose Jewish population had been increased by refugees from persecutions elsewhere until Jews formed the third largest ethnic group in that Mesopotamian land. In time, three distinct Jewish academies flourished there, and also a Sanhedrin, a rival to the great council set up at Usha in the Galilee.

Babylonian scholars called *Amoraim* (expounders) worked at "clarifying the clarifier"—that is, at elucidating the Mishnah. Their additional commentary is called the *Gemara* or "learning." The two together—Mishnah plus Gemara—are known as the *Talmud*, an old Hebrew word signifying "research."

The Babylonian Talmud was completed finally soon after 500 C.E. It did not remain static even then. Great Hebrew scholars such as Maimonides, Rashi, and Caro, who lived much later, continued to interpret and expand the scope of the Talmud in order that it might better serve the changed needs of their own times. The great Talmudic traditions of study, interpretation, and modification have not truly been terminated even yet.

The Jerusalem Talmud, sometimes called the Talmud of Palestine, was, on the other hand, rounded out as early as the middle of the fourth century. Authorities consider it less complete and admirable than the Babylonian Talmud. This is hardly to be wondered at, in view of Roman restrictions that hampered the scholars who compiled the Palestinian Talmud. Nevertheless, students of the history of the land that became Israel find much of value in the pages of that earlier and briefer Talmud.

9

ISRAEL UNDER BYZANTINES AND PERSIANS

(TO ABOUT 570)

Many nations encircled me . . .
They encircled me all around . . .
They swarmed about me like bees.

They were quenched like a fire among thorns.
In the name of the Lord I overcame them.
Though the Lord has chastened me
    yet he has not given me over to death.

—FROM PSALM 118

Conditions eased somewhat under Diocletian, emperor from 284 to 305 C.E. Then Constantine became emperor, and during his first dozen years tolerance was shown to all religions in the empire, including that of the Jews. Later Constantine took two related steps which substantially changed conditions for that time and the future: he chose Christianity as the religion for himself and his empire, and he moved his capital from pagan Rome to eastern Byzantium, which was then renamed Constantinople in his honor. Today it is the famous and beautiful city of Istanbul.

Once again Jews were barred from living in Jerusalem. They even had to pay an admission fee to enter the city each year on the 9th of Ab to mourn the destruction of the Temple. They were not deprived of Roman citizenship, however.

By 324 C.E. the new Christianized, easternized, and Greek-language-using Byzantine regime was fully in control of the land where the gentle "troublemaker" Jesus of Nazareth had lived and died. His life, three centuries before, led in this period to intensive searches for traces and relics in and near Jerusalem. Helena, mother of Constantine, toured this new "holy land," everywhere asking to be shown sites and remains linked with the life of Jesus. Orders were issued to destroy the pagan temples standing there. When the old Jerusalem shrine to Aphrodite-Venus was torn down, Helena exultantly announced that there she had found the very tomb in which the body of Jesus had rested between his crucifixion and his resurrection. There, or nearby, Helena claimed also to have found "the true cross" itself.

Imposing Christian churches were erected to commemorate these miraculous finds: in Jerusalem, the churches of the Holy Sepulchre and the Eleona; in Bethlehem, the Church of the Nativity. The same Syria Palestine that earlier Roman rulers regarded as a trouble spot and source of sedition now became a sacred jewel in the ornate crown of the emperor who ruled in luxury in Constantinople-Byzantium.

Again pilgrims journeyed far to visit Jerusalem, but now they were Christians seeking the spots sanctified by the life of Jesus, not Jews come to worship at the great Temple dating back to Solomon and Herod. The Jews who had so long regarded Jerusalem and the Israel around it as their "promised land" were now pushed aside. The promise may have been given to their ancestors, but the presence and the power in that land were now the Christianized Roman-Greek authorities.

The oppression of the remaining Jews became still more severe under the following emperor, Constantius. Church law did not allow Christians to eat with Jews, and Christian women could not marry Jews. Christian men might still wed Jewish women, however, for it was hoped that the latter would become converts to Christianity.

Other new prohibitions kept Jews from owning Christian slaves. Much of the farming and the textile-weaving industry of the land had depended on slave labor. Now many Jews were forced to sell their land; others lost their weaving enterprises. Constantius used many harsh means to prevent any growth in the Jewish population.

Unendurable repressions again led to revolt, this time in 351 C.E., when the empire was busy making war against Persia. This uprising seems to have started at Sepphoris, where Jews overwhelmed the imperial garrison and took their weapons. From there the revolt spread to other centers, including Tiberias and Lod. Legions of the empire marched in, and during 352 C.E. the old pattern was repeated: widespread killings, drastic punishments, and worsened conditions for the defeated Jews.

The darkness lightened a little when Julian was briefly emperor, 361–363 C.E. He had been reared as a Christian and had studied the Bible extensively but had been repelled by the incessant quarrels and splits within the Christian churches. He went back to paganism, at first in secret, then openly, becoming known to Christians by a bitter title: Julian the Apostate.

The Jews, however, found him a friend and an admirer of their faith. Under his rule their crushing taxes were reduced and their lost civil rights restored. Finding that the Jews had given up the ancient custom of animal sacrifice and were worshipping in local gatherings or synagogues, Julian authorized the rebuilding of the Temple. He appointed his friend Alypsius of Antioch to help in the project and instructed the governors of Palestine itself and Syria to the north to aid also. Many workers began to clear the rubble that cluttered the site of the former Temple, from which great numbers of the best stones had been taken to build Christian churches. It was spring of 363 C.E. when work began toward the new Temple.

Among the Jews themselves, attitudes seem to have differed. Some responded with joy and hope. Others, more literal in their beliefs, expected a Messiah to appear before a new Temple could be undertaken, and there was no Messiah in sight. Soon enough, however, the Temple question ceased to be an issue. Repeated troubles plagued the work: fires, explosions of underground gas, even an earthquake. Finally the project was abandoned.

The Christians called these difficulties miraculous warnings to the Jews and proof that God favored Christianity. The lurid rumor arose that Julian meant to build a prison for Christians on the site, instead of a Temple. The final blow to Temple prospects came when Julian was killed by an arrow during a battle with the Persians in June 363 C.E. Some said the arrow came from a bow aimed by a Christian in his own army.

After Julian's death, harsh and restrictive laws were again imposed on the Jews in the "promised land." It was not long afterward that one of the great Church "Fathers," St. Jerome, reported that Jews in Palestine had dwindled to a tenth of their former number.

Under Theodosius, who was emperor from 379 to 395 C.E., Christianity was elevated. It now became the official state religion of the entire empire. Previously, under Constantine and others, it had been but an "allowed" or *licit* religion.

Before the end of the fourth century c.e., Palestine had become largely Christian in population, and the ancient Jewish center of Jerusalem had become the religious focus of the Christian world, perhaps even more prominently than Rome today is the focus for the Catholic Christian world.

About this time a fierce and far-traveled Asiatic nomadic people, the Huns, invaded the eastern Roman empire. Refugees fleeing before them crowded into Palestine. For a time it seemed that the Huns might even force their way into Palestine itself. During this critical period many Jewish villages disappeared, especially in the southern part of what is now Israel. Even in the north, where Jews were more numerous, they formed only about 15 percent of the whole population. They were a downtrodden and largely downhearted group. Many migrated to Babylon, now the chief center for Jewish learning. Others went elsewhere, far from Israel.

Surviving Jews in Palestine managed as best they could. Oddly enough, many earned a meager living as guides, taking the new crop of Christian pilgrims to the holy places linked with the Old Testament. The ban against Jewish entry into Jerusalem itself continued. Officially, Jews might enter that city only to mourn on the 9th of Ab, anniversary of the Temple's destruction. They often bribed soldiers to let them pray at the site of the Temple. There they wept and bewailed the loss that never ceased to give pain. St. Jerome, mentioned earlier, told of seeing these mourners —a miserable, pale, ragged group, lamenting their lost Temple— repeatedly solicited by the cynical Roman guards to pay again for the privilege of remaining a while longer.

In the fifth century c.e., the Christianizing of Palestine proceeded further. The Christian pilgrims came from lands as distant as Gaul (now France), Spain, Italy, Arabia, Mesopotamia, and even India. Some wealthy Romans chose to make Jerusalem their place of residence. Others went to Bethlehem, Ashkelon, or Gaza. Monks arrived in numbers. So too did solitary hermits. Near and far, new Christian churches were built, sometimes as many as two to five in a single village. Most of these were later destroyed during the long Moslem rule of the land, but their remnants can often be found, many times with floors richly decorated in Byzantine mosaic work.

Also, the collecting and selling of Christian religious relics increased. Most of these were removed from Palestine, and those that found their way to Europe helped to generate the fanaticism that eventually led to the Crusades and brought European armies to Palestine about 600 years later.

The Byzantine Emperor Theodosius II could not get along with his wife, Eudocia, so in 444 C.E. he sent her to live in Palestine, where she remained for sixteen years, until her death. She was a dedicated Christian, but she had been born a pagan and was not hostile to the Jewish people. Thanks to her influence, Jews and Samaritans were able to live in Aelia, as the Byzantines still called Jerusalem. Even so, the Jews were granted only limited citizenship, being denied the right to serve as officials or agents of the government.

The laws of Theodosius II allowed neither the building of new synagogues nor the repair and enlargement of old ones. In secret, however, this ban was ignored. Later excavations reveal that modest or meager fronts sometimes hid ample or even elaborate synagogue interiors. The decorations within, clearly influenced by prevailing Byzantine art, included many an image of animal or human figures.

While synagogues were restricted, the power of the Christian church grew. Jerusalem was raised to the level of a Christian "see," thus making it superior in church matters to Caesarea, though that remained the site of the Byzantine civil government of the region.

Jews were not alone in being persecuted in this period. Pagans, Christian dissidents or heretics, and Samaritans were also heavily handicapped. Some of the stringent laws against Judaism probably give a clue to its basic appeal. The Jewish doctrines of mercy and eventual liberation for slaves caused many of them, once freed, to wish to become Jews. The Church Fathers countered this in two ways: by making it a capital offense for onetime Christians to convert to Judaism, and by not allowing Jews to own slaves, though Christians were not similarly limited.

Although Christian women were forbidden by law to marry Jewish men, word seems to have got around that Jews made good, steady husbands, providing well for their families and seeing to the education of their children. The Church edict against such marriages would hardly have been needed had there been no tendency for them to take place.

Justinian, Byzantine emperor from 527 to 565 C.E., was an enthusiastic builder and student of architecture. He searched Palestine for sites and ideas for ever more impressive churches. Jerusalem has never since had so many churches as under Justinian. It was also during his rule that Jews were barred from appearing as court witnesses against Christians. Thus the Jews were denied equal justice. In one way or another they were made to suffer for their stubborn refusal to convert to the powerful new religion named for their co-religionist, the humble Jew of Nazareth, Jesus the Christ.

After Justinian, the fabled splendor of the Byzantine empire began to dim. Its resources were drained in increasing struggles with the Persians. The majority of the residents of Palestine became weary of Byzantine rule, for times were hard, wages depressed, prices rising. Byzantine administration was rigid, hidebound, cumbersome. The Jews had an additional cause for resentment: the Byzantine policy of seeking to force them to convert to Christianity.

Many Jews who lived in eastern communities outside Byzantine rule served in the Persian armies and so fought the regime in Constantinople. An appeal was issued seeking the aid even of the Jews of Palestine. A very wealthy man by the name of Benjamin used his fortune to recruit and arm Jewish volunteers from Tiberias, Nazareth, and the Galilean hill towns. Possibly as many as twenty thousand Jews were thus mobilized. This estimate suggests the participation of a large part of the remaining Jewish population, now down to about 250,000, compared with some

800,000 at the close of the great Bar Kochba revolt against Rome.

It has been estimated also that at the beginning of the seventh century c.e. not more than half a million Jews in all were alive within the borders of the somewhat diminished Roman empire. There had been some three million Jews under Roman dominion prior to the First Revolt and the destruction of the Temple in 70 c.e.

All of this made easier the later conquest of Palestine by the Persians under their King Chosroes II. In 614 c.e. they swept south through Lebanon and Syria, taking Damascus and storming Jerusalem. They received some aid from Jewish guerrilla fighters within the land itself. The taking of Jerusalem exacted a toll of lives estimated all the way from 24,000 to about four times that many. Most of the churches and monasteries of the city, including the Church of the Holy Sepulchre, were burned to the ground.

The Christian patriarch Zacharias became one of the many captives carried off into exile. Besides the prisoners, the Persians also carried off the relic of the "true cross" that Constantine's mother, Helena, had discovered in the fourth century.

Grateful at first for Jewish aid, the Persians appointed Jews as administrators in Jerusalem. Many Jews now returned to live within the city of the lost Temple, and also in Bethlehem. Again plans for rebuilding the Temple were discussed. But this stage lasted only three years. Realizing that the Jews were only a minority in the land, the Persian rulers turned over local control to Christians. The situation of the Jews steadily grew worse until the end of Persian rule, which took place only some fourteen years after it had begun.

That end came when Heraclius, Byzantine emperor from 610 to 641 c.e., invaded Persia. He rescued Christian captives, recovered the relic of the "true cross," and even regained control over Palestine itself. His triumphal entry into Jerusalem took place March 23, 630 c.e. Heraclius passed through the legendary Golden Gate in the eastern wall around what had been the Temple site, and on foot he bore the sacred relic back to its place in the Church of the Holy Sepulchre.

Heraclius had been aided by some Jewish guerrillas who were

embittered by the broken promises of the Persians and attracted by new promises from Heraclius. However, once Byzantine rule was again firmly in control of the land, the Jews underwent ordeals all too familiar from the past. Again they were forbidden to live in or near Jerusalem. Elsewhere in the land they suffered other harsh penalties. Many fled in fear. Some took refuge in the Judean mountains and wilderness; others escaped to Egypt.

A strange story is linked with astrology and superstition. Heraclius is said to have been warned by astrologers that Byzantium would be defeated by circumcised people. He assumed this must mean the Jews and so was the more willing to have them persecuted or even slain. Before long Byzantium was beaten, but its circumcised conquerors were the Moslems, not the Jews.

It was not the stars but the festering internal weaknesses of the Byzantine empire that made it an inevitable loser to this dynamic new power out of the desert—a power that for nearly twelve centuries was to dominate the historic bit of land that became the Israel of today.

10

THE PROPHET FROM THE DESERT: ISLAM ARISES

(TO ABOUT 800)

Blessed be the Lord, my rock,
who trains my hands for war,
my fingers for battle;
My refuge and my fortress,
my stronghold, my deliverer;
My shield in whom I trust.

—FROM PSALM 144

Around 570 C.E. there was born in Mecca, in what is now western Saudi Arabia near the Red Sea, a remarkable man whose influence is still felt strongly to this day. He was to leave an indelible mark on Palestine and its people. Countless legends have grown up around the life of the prophet Mohammed (570–632).* He has been called the most significant figure in medieval history. He and his followers did indeed change the religious, political, and geographical picture of the entire East, the Mediterranean area, and Europe.

Mohammed belonged to the clan of the Zoraishites, part of the Quraish tribe. He came to hate their worship of many idols and in its place founded a new religion based on one God, like that of the Jews. Its name of *Islam* means "submission" (to God's will). Mohammed claimed that this religion came to him in a series of divine revelations. He had been a camel driver, then a merchant in caravans on the trade routes between southern Arabia, Syria, and Mediterranean ports. Thus he came into contact with Jews and also with Christians. Both religions influenced him, the Jewish more than the Christian.

Jews, in fact, had been moving slowly into Arabia, reversing the ancient migrations from the desert into Israel. By the fifth and sixth centuries C.E., Jews, fleeing the grinding wars between the Byzantines and Persians, reached Arabia in considerable numbers

---

* Many of these legends are recorded in *Temple Beyond Time* by Mina C. and H. Arthur Klein (New York, 1970).

from both Palestine and Syria. They were a literate, even relatively learned people. Before their arrival, Arabia's inhabitants had been either wandering Bedouin tribes in the desert, or the Quraish tribes of the coastal areas and trading routes. By the seventh century c.e., Jews formed a substantial part of the population in Arabia and had helped to develop its commerce, industry, and arts. They are credited with introducing there the valuable date palm, a tree whose fruits have benefited many generations. It was the Arabs, apparently, who first gave the Jews a revealing and revered name, "The People of the Book."

During this era and many others later, friendly and cooperative relations existed between Jews and Arabs, both the authentic original Arabs who were native to what the Romans called "Arabia," and the many other peoples who came from elsewhere but were known as Arabs because of their use of the Arabian language.

The great and sacred book into which Mohammed poured his messages, his warnings, his fantasies, was called the *Koran*, meaning "recitation." It had indeed been recited or dictated, for Mohammed could not read or write and used a scribe, or secretary, to take down his sayings and decisions. Late in life he is said to have learned to read by "revelation" rather than by instruction. The Koran is studded with direct influences and adaptations from the Jewish Bible and from the Talmud also.

Mohammed adopted basic Jewish principles and practices: fasting, circumcision, and the ban on eating the flesh of the pig. The Founding Fathers and prophets of the Jews also were adopted by the new religion of the *Moslems* or *Muslims*, which words signify "the surrendering ones" or "those who have made peace with God."

Peace on earth was not typical of the first centuries of the growth and spread of Islam, but this religion took deep roots, and in almost every part of the world where it once prevailed, people today still practice it. About 15 percent of the world's population—fully half a billion people—today are Moslems believing that "there is no God but Allah" and that Mohammed is his prophet, or at any rate his principal prophet. Thus, like the Jews who worship only one God—the Moslems also worship one God, whom they call *Allah*.

Mohammed, like most Arabs, admired the literacy, learning, and industry of the Jews. Repeatedly he tried to win Jewish support for his new movement, especially among Jews living in and around Medina (Yathrib), a city said to have been founded by Jews fleeing into Arabia from wars in the west. However, those Jews declined to acclaim him as a prophet or to aid him in his battles against the pagans. They aligned themselves mostly with the pagan tribes around Medina. In disappointment and bitterness, Mohammed discarded much that was Jewish in his new religion. For example, at first his followers, like the Jews among them, were taught to pray facing in the direction of Jerusalem. But in 623 C.E. Mohammed changed the direction of prayer to Mecca, his own birthplace.

Nevertheless, Jerusalem remained sacred to the Moslem faith, and even now is regarded by it as the holiest place on earth, after Mecca and Medina. A colorful section of the Koran tells how Mohammed, astride a miraculous steed, was transported one night from Mecca to the site of the former Temple in Jerusalem, with the great angel Gabriel as his guide. There Mohammed is said to have led in prayer the earlier prophet-patriarchs Abraham, Moses, and Jesus, after which, from the sacred rock which had stood under the Ark in the Holy of Holies of Solomon's Temple, Mohammed ascended to the "seventh heaven" in the full radiance of Allah—then returned safely to the rock, and to his own bed in Mecca, all before morning. In commemoration of this night ride, later Moslems built and maintained over that very rock the beautiful octagonal shrine called the Dome of the Rock which still stands on Mount Moriah in Old Jerusalem.

Mohammed at first had chosen the Jewish sabbath, Saturday, as the day of rest for his followers also. Only later did he shift that day to Friday for Moslems. His break with the Jews also took far more terrible forms. When he became a military leader and ruler of masses of faithful and zealous followers, he persecuted Jewish communities in the regions he controlled. During 627–629 C.E. his forces nearly wiped out three such Jewish groups.

Some were faced with exile and the confiscation of their property. Others were given the choice of death or enforced conversion to the Moslem religion. With the help of wealth confiscated from Jews, Mohammed raised a force of ten thousand fighters, marched against his birthplace Mecca, and there defeated the powerful Quraish, the Arab tribe that had refused to accept his message.

His abilities as warrior, administrator, and organizer were enormous. Starting with almost nothing, he created an empire during the decade before his death in 632 c.e. All of Arabia and parts of North Africa and western Asia later acknowledged Moslem rule and supremacy. Nor did Mohammed's followers cease to spread the new faith by the sword after their prophet died. Their leaders in the later holy wars were called *caliphs,* from an Arab word meaning "successor" (to Mohammed).

Within the hundred years preceding the middle of the eighth century c.e., the followers of Mohammed dominated half the known world, including large parts of Asia and northern Africa. By 711 c.e. they were established in Spain. In the west they were halted only by the Pyrenees Mountains and French resistance. In the east they were checked for a time by the Byzantine empire, ruled from Constantinople.

By one of the many mislabelings of history, all these conquering Moslems became known as "Arabs," though they came not only from Arabia but also from Persia, Syria, Egypt, and elsewhere in the great new empire of Islam. Confusion as to the correct meaning and scope of the term "Arab" remains today with regard to ancestry and even to language usage.

The thrust and force of Islam were felt early in what we now call Israel. Even during Mohammed's life, his followers had attacked the site of Eilat, southernmost city of modern Israel, and had won a treaty from the Byzantine administrator of that region.

The ensuing Islamic conquest of all Palestine and Syria was not difficult. The populace there seems generally to have welcomed the invaders, for the Christian powers in the land had become divided and were hostile to each other. Most of the Syrian Christians rejected the church supported by the Byzantine government and adhered instead to a branch known as the Monophysites. They were glad to be rid of the Byzantine rule. To most of the Syrians, the Arabs from Arabia seemed like brothers.

After Syria was safely in hand and Jerusalem taken, the Moslem forces moved south and conducted a lengthy siege of the important administrative city of Caesarea on the coast. It fell only after several years, and then through the action of a traitor who revealed a secret way into the city.

The first caliph, Abu Bekr, had died in 638 c.e. and had been followed by a remarkable leader known as Caliph Omar (Umar Abu ibn el-Khattab, 582–644). He had been a personal friend of Mohammed, one of his earliest converts, and was a devout, even fanatical, follower of the faith. It was he who had achieved the peaceful surrender of Jerusalem after a long siege. The city had been ruled by the Christian patriarch Sophronius, who was left in charge by the Byzantines. Sophronius sought to preserve the city from destruction and massacre, and at the same time to protect Christian interests.

The legends of Omar's first entry into Jerusalem are many and fascinating. He asked to be shown the site of the Temple from which Mohammed had made his great nighttime ascent to the seventh heaven. Sophronius, however, pretended that the site had been forgotten, for he feared that the Moslems would build a house of worship there or, even worse, return the site to the Jews.

Omar persisted and finally found the place. It was in a shockingly filthy state. Romans, Byzantines, and Christians long had used it as a dump for garbage and refuse to demonstrate their contempt for the troublesome and stubborn Jews. Omar had the site cleared, and even, according to one story, used his own robes to help in the work. At the south end of the Temple platform on Mount Moriah he built a very simple structure for Moslem worship, near the place where the splendid palace of King Solomon had once stood.

The contrast is interesting. Solomon had sought the utmost richness and display for his time. Omar was an austere, almost puritanical, person. He disapproved of luxury and material splendor in any form. Only later did the great caliphs indulge in luxury.

Under Omar, Jerusalem was spared from destruction. He allowed the Christians to keep their places of worship and their rituals. He required only that the taxes and tributes formerly paid to the Byzantines be paid instead to the new Moslem government. Omar—unlike so many before him—did allow Jews to live in Jerusalem.

The new Moslem regime in practice permitted Jews to return not only to their sacred city but to all of what is now Israel. As an indication of the new trend, the body which then had the highest legislative authority for the Jews—the council of heads of academies, often called the *Geonim*—moved from Tiberias to Jerusalem itself. This council is said to have exercised more influence on the Jews of the land than even the so-called *Exilarchs*, or chief Jews, exercised in Babylon to the east. It was Caliph Omar, in fact, who, when his forces conquered Mesopotamia, restored the position of Exilarch of the Jews, in recognition perhaps of the aid given to the Moslems by many of the Jews of that region. The Jewish governing council continued active in Jerusalem until the middle of the eleventh century c.e., about fifty years before the Crusades.

Relatively little damaged by the Moslem conquest, the land was now reorganized by the new regime. Being warriors, rather than bureaucrats as the Byzantine officials had been before them, the Moslems parceled out Syria and Palestine into military districts, each one called a *jund*, meaning "army." There was a "Filastin" jund, with its capital first at Lod, then at Ramla; and an "Urdunn" jund, ruled from Tiberias. The actual lower officers who performed the day-to-day administration continued to be Byzantines, and Greek, the language of the Byzantine empire, continued to be spoken throughout the land.

Gradually, through the years, Moslem control increased. Nevertheless, Christian pilgrims were permitted to visit holy places such as Bethlehem and Jerusalem. The Arabs altered the name of Jerusalem in several interesting ways. Usually they called it *Al-Quds*, meaning "holiness," but sometimes they called it *Iliya*, for it had been Aelia under Hadrian and later. Also they gave it the poetic title of *al Balat*, meaning "palace," and even *Beit al-*

Maqdis, which related to the Hebrew name for the Temple, the glory of the lost Jerusalem of the Jews.

In the Islamic empire, Jews in general found life better than it had been earlier under Christian rule. The seventh century C.E. had been an era of terror and forced conversion for them, especially in pre-Moorish Spain. Now, within a generation or two after the death of Mohammed, Islamic treatment of the Jews improved, especially in Spain, Egypt, and Islamic Asia. The Arabs came to look up to the Jews as part of their intellectual community, along with the Greeks and the Persians. On the other hand, the Arabs tended to look down on the Christians, as they did also on the Turks and the Chinese to the east.

From about 700 to 1000 C.E. there flourished a period of Jewish eminence and achievement that has been called a "golden age." In medicine, mathematics, science, scholarship, philosophy, linguistics, government, and even military administration, leading Jews made enormous contributions to the Islamic empire. The five hundred years following this period brought a decline to the Islamic empire, however, and as it faded, so too faded that "golden age" for its Jews.

In the land we know as Israel, Byzantine rule had much reduced the size of the Jewish communities. Now, in the Islamic era, these communities began to develop and to thrive. In Jerusalem itself the caliph allowed seventy Jewish families to become residents. Their numbers were increased by a large group who called themselves "Mourners for Zion." These remained in the city to pray and to mourn for the Temple destroyed in 70 C.E. Between about 637 and 1009 C.E., Jews were allowed to ascend above the base of the Western Wall to what had been the Temple platform, and there to pray where once the great gates and the altar of the Temple itself had stood. Increasingly also they prayed at the remnant of the Western Wall itself. To pay for the privilege of praying, they were obliged to clean up the rubbish and refuse in the Temple area.

Jewish learning developed in other centers of Israel. Tiberias in the Galilee, though no longer on a par with Jerusalem as the principal center of sacred studies, did continue active and important. So too did Haifa, Ashkelon, and Gaza along the Mediterranean coast. Jews also returned in numbers to Aleppo, Tyre, and Tripolis in what is now Syria but was then part of the Holy Land. Damascus, too, became a substantial Jewish center.

Jewish communities far beyond the limits of that remembered Holy Land sent contributions of money to foster Jewish studies and settlements there. That tradition—the financial support of Jews within the land of Israel by fellow-Jews in the Diaspora, or great worldwide scattering—continued through the centuries and helped to make possible the founding and growth of the present state of Israel.

Jews lived in and near Jerusalem itself and continued to live there until the disaster of the taking of that city by the Crusaders —and this despite the rise of rivalries and dissensions within the ranks of the ruling Moslems. Those rivalries and shifts produced the succession of caliphs called the "Omayyad dynasty," which held control from about 661 C.E. until some ninety years later, with fourteen caliphs ruling during that time.

Of particular importance was the caliphate of Abd al-Malik, beginning in 685 C.E. He was a poet and a lover of learning, and— like many another intellectual Arab—he was proud of the richness and subtlety of the Arab language. Something of the same love of language beauty and purity carried over to intellectual Jews in the land that became Israel. During their days of decline under the Byzantine regime they had spoken a mixture of Hebrew (from their past), Chaldee (from Mesopotamia), and imperfect Greek. Within half a century after the Arab conquest, leading Jews were writing and translating into Arabic works of science and literature. They likewise developed a passion for a pure, uncontaminated Hebrew and a determination to rejuvenate this, the language of their own Bible.

Al-Malik was a great builder, and his greatest single project was the lovely Dome of the Rock on the Temple platform of Mount Moriah, Jerusalem. This beautiful edifice, sometimes called mistakenly the Mosque of Omar, stands today as one of the finest examples of Islamic architecture and decoration. In it can be traced elements of the best of the Hellenic, Persian, and Byzantine styles. Begun in 687 and finished four years later, it is still one of the loveliest of many memorable structures in modern Israel.

Caliph al-Malik hoped by means of this beautiful new shrine to lure from Mecca and Medina some of the thousands of Moslem pilgrims who flocked there each year. Those cities were then under the rule of a rival caliph, typical of the splits that had developed in the house of Islam. The Dome of the Rock never did compete successfully with that other great attraction, the *Kaaba*, which houses the sacred meteor stone of Mecca. But the Dome of the Rock and the nearby el Aksa mosque on the Temple platform at Jerusalem remain holy sites for Islam and sights of memorable beauty and dignity for travelers of all faiths and philosophies.

Jews of Jerusalem played a part in the creation and care of the Dome of the Rock. They were among the staff of three hundred who kept it beautiful. They did such work as sweeping and cleaning, making vessels of glass and plates for the countless lamps which provided the light that at night radiated from the gorgeous windows on the eight sides of the Dome. All these caretakers of the Dome were exempted from paying taxes—a valuable concession.

After 705 C.E., two sons of al-Malik ruled the land that became Israel: al-Walid as caliph, and Suleiman as governor (not to be confused with the more famous Suleiman the Magnificent). Al-Walid became the greatest of the builders of the Omayyad dynasty. It was he who completed the original el Aksa mosque mentioned earlier. The later el Aksa stands today at the southern end of the Temple platform where once had stood the simple Moslem house of worship built by Omar.

Jerusalem, though sacred to the three great religions—Jewish, Christian, and Moslem—was not the capital of the district. Under Suleiman a new capital for Palestine was begun on the sand dunes south of Lod. It was given the name Ramla, from the Arab word *raml* for "sand." It was further enlarged when Suleiman became caliph following the death of his brother.

The land we call Israel included both Jews and Christians

whose ancestors had lived there for as long as could be remembered, or as far back as records existed. Both Jews and Christians paid special taxes, which, however, were not heavy. The Omayyad caliphs were tolerant and respected the religious convictions of their subjects. The Jewish rabbis represented their people in dealings with the Omayyad officials, and the Christian priests represented theirs. Conditions were good enough to attract into the land some additional Arab tribes, mostly from the southern part of Arabia.

About the middle of the eighth century c.e., the Omayyad rulers were replaced by their rivals, the Abbasids, descendants of an uncle of Mohammed. These new caliphs were less interested in the Palestine-Syria region, and moved their capital from Damascus to the Mesopotamian city of Bagdad, in what is now Iraq.

Changes in commerce and government policy more and more shifted the passage of important goods from the trade routes through the Negev south of Jerusalem to the Mesopotamian region. No longer was the great Negev region an important link between southern Arabia and the Far East on the one hand, and the Mediterranean ports on the other. By the mid-eighth century c.e., the Negev roads were deteriorating and becoming deserted. By the end of the eleventh century the Negev had become sparsely populated and completely devoid of caravan trade. It is hard to imagine the Negev as anything but a deserted wilderness. However, there were centuries during which it was a busy and relatively well-populated region.

Harun al-Rashid, who ruled from 786 to 809 c.e., is today the best known of the Abbasids. He was, in fact, the caliph around whom the *Thousand and One Nights* or *Arabian Nights* tales were assembled. Not mentioned in those fictions but sadly factual were the oppressive laws in force for a time under him. Jews were forced to wear yellow badges, Christians blue ones. This was, incidentally, also the era of the great Charlemagne (742–814), powerful Christian king of the Franco-German region of Europe. Friendly relations were established between Charlemagne and Caliph al-Rashid, with exchanges of flattering messages and gifts.

This led the latter to permit the building of a number of Christian churches in the Holy Land. Pilgrims began to visit there from the western Roman Catholic countries, in addition to those from the eastern, Byzantine Christian lands.

The increased flow of visitors brought back into Europe a greater awareness of the riches and strategic importance of the country. This growing awareness climaxed, after three centuries, in the launching of the Crusades, so disastrous for the Jews in Palestine.

Under the reign of al-Mamun (813–833), son of Caliph al-Rashid, religious tolerance was restored. Jewish synagogues by the hundreds were active, and thousands of Christian churches, monasteries, and shrines operated in the caliph's realm.

11

STRANGE SECTS
IN JUDAISM, AND
ISLAMIC DYNASTIES

(TO ABOUT 1075)

. . . the enemy pursues me,
  he has crushed my life to the ground;
he has left me dwelling in the dark
  like those long dead.

. . . my spirit is faint within me,
  my heart within me is appalled.

I remember the days of old;
  I meditate on all your doings. . . .
I stretch out my hands to you;
  my soul thirsts for you like parched land.

Hasten to answer me, O Lord,
  for my spirit fails me.

—FROM PSALM 143

J ews in the land that became Israel fared better under the Moslem rule than they had for a long time. This new period also brought internal ferment and differences in point of view between large groups of Jews outside and inside that land.

From time to time during the eighth century C.E., Jewish sects appeared which rejected the Talmud, calling it oppressive and tyrannical. In its place they urged a return to the greater simplicity and purity of the Torah, the basic books of the Bible.

Early in that century Serene, living in what is now Syria, announced that he was the Messiah, with a mission to cast the Moslems out of the Holy Land. He urged also that the Talmud be discarded and with it the dietary laws and other restrictions accepted by orthodox Jews of the time. He gained thousands of followers, but he was arrested by the reigning caliph, Yazed II, and turned over to the Jewish authorities to be punished.

About thirty years later in Persia another religious resistance group appeared, when Obadiah Abu Isa, a Jew, called also for a return to the simpler precepts of the Bible. About ten thousand Persian Jews became his followers. He was a soldier as well as a reformer, and he died at the head of his troops in 755 C.E., leaving a sect, the Isavites, whose remnants survived until late in the tenth century.

The most important dissident movement, however, was founded by Anan ben David in Bagdad. It was to endure until the present under the name of *Karaism*—derived from words meaning "to read."

Anan and his followers in 767 c.e. defied the Geonim, the Jewish religious authorities, or "elders," in Mesopotamia. He was imprisoned by the caliph, but managed to get away to Palestine. Once in Jerusalem, he founded his own synagogue, and from there his sect spread into Syria, Egypt, and southeastern Europe.

Like the Isavites, Anan and his followers rejected Talmudic rules and complexities. They accepted only the Bible as the authority for right Jewish conduct. Hence Karaism—"to read"— meant really reading the Torah (Bible) rather than the far longer and more intricate Talmud. Anan's views have been called a return to the principles of the Sadducees, a concept implying that the Talmud was mainly an outgrowth of Pharisee influences.

To Anan and his followers, Jesus was a great Jewish prophet who had resisted the restrictions imposed by the rabbis of his own time but had not intended to found any new religion apart from Judaism. Some of the rules laid down by the Karaites were milder than those of the Talmud, but others were a good deal stricter. For example, they observed more days of fasting. They altered the customary dietary laws, shunning the meat of all animals except the deer and the pigeon. Doctors of medicine were forbidden, for only the Lord healed. The Karaites had special laws for marriage, the Sabbath, and other vital areas of human life. Within the Karaites as a whole further subdivisions existed, each with special rules and interpretations of its own.

In the light of the history we are tracing, probably the most significant Karaite idea was that all Jews ought to return to live in the land now called Israel. The Talmud, they taught, was valid only for Jews in the Diaspora, or scattering, but not needed for those who lived in their own proper "promised land."

The Karaite movement might have splintered completely and disappeared early but for Benjamin Nahavendi, who was active in it some fifty years after Anan himself had died. This later Karaite leader toned down many of the most severe rules and simplified Karaite thinking. Thus strengthened, the movement continued to spread and to gain influence among Jews until the tenth century. After that, various Karaite groups disagreed and quarreled, until by the start of the twelfth century their influence had all but vanished.

Though it seemed for a time to be disruptive, Karaism had its values. It forced the Talmudic rabbis to be more alert and kept them from bogging down in outworn traditions. It led to inquiry and greater independence of thinking. Also, it stimulated the study of the Hebrew language, for both Karaites and their foes turned to that language to find evidence to support their views. Without the stimulus of Karaite controversies, the revival of Hebrew literature might have been long delayed.

Even as these lines are written, a small group of Karaites, about twelve thousand in all, still live. Most of them are in the Soviet Union, but a number have returned to the modern land of Israel. In the eyes of its all-embracing "Law of Return," they—like all Jews—are regarded not as alien immigrants, but rather as repatriates returning to a land to whose citizenship they have an ancient and honorable claim. Thus, after some 1,200 years, Karaites are being absorbed into the swift-moving daily life of the land which their founders taught should be the only place of residence for all the world's Jews.

Saadiah ben Joseph (882–942 C.E.), sometimes called Saadia Gaon, was born in upper Egypt at a time when there were probably not more than half a million Jews alive in the world, their numbers having been drastically reduced by warfare, massacres, and persecutions. Saadia became a learned man and a wise one. A stout supporter of Talmudic traditions, he was well versed also in the tenets of the various dissident Jewish movements, and even had a broad knowledge of Mohammedanism. He was able to refute the ideas of those dissident sects by the arguments set forth in his widely esteemed writings.

So skilled was Saadia in Arabic that he translated the Bible into that language and issued a Hebrew dictionary and a Hebrew grammar written in Arabic. However, he was not a retiring or sedentary scholar, for he traveled in Palestine, Syria, and Babylon, finally becoming head of the respected Jewish academy at Sura, Babylon. He is credited with laying the foundations for Jewish philosophy in the medieval period, and some of his views are reflected in the philosophical works of the great Maimonides, who wrote in the twelfth century.

A few years after Saadia died, the famous Sura academy was closed. It was never reopened. By the mid-eleventh century the other Babylonian Jewish academies and the Geonate had become ineffectual. They vanished utterly in the following centuries.

The new centers of Jewish learning and authority were now found in the West—especially in Moorish Spain and North Africa. More and more the center of gravity of Jewish studies and speculations was shifting toward the Atlantic and into Europe itself. Yet despite the decline in the East, and in Palestine in particular, that area's small Jewish population was continually added to by religious Jews who came to live, or perhaps merely to die, in the land of their fathers.

In 877 C.E., Ahmad ibn-Tulun, a freed slave, became governor of Egypt. He declared his realm independent of the Abbasid caliph in Bagdad. From then on, the history of the land we call Israel is linked with events in Egypt as well as in Syria. The Tulunid dynasty lasted until 905 C.E. About thirty years later Egypt again became dominant in Palestine, as the Ikshid dynasty began its rule of Egypt.

Such internal Islamic conflicts helped to win small concessions for the Jews in Jerusalem. About the middle of the tenth century they got permission to enter the longed-for former site of the Temple itself on their religious holidays. They were also allowed to go from gate to gate in the walls surrounding the Temple mount, and even to pray beside those gates "in a loud voice." Moreover, they were permitted to erect a synagogue not far from the famous "Wailing Wall," wet by centuries of Jewish tears.

Within Jerusalem, friction increased between Moslems and Christians. In 935 C.E. the former outraged the latter by building a mosque in the very courtyard of the Church of the Holy Sepulchre. About thirty years later, fires set by fanatical Moslem mobs damaged that church among many others. John, the Christian patriarch of Jerusalem, perished in the flames. Alarmed, the Christians called for outside aid.

From Constantinople, warriors of the Byzantine empire began a victorious march toward Jerusalem. They were headed by the Byzantine emperor himself. It was his sudden death in 976 C.E., when in sight of the sacred city, that put an end to that campaign.

A new Islamic dynasty—the Fatimids—had now come to power. Their governors and officials were constantly shifted about in Palestine and Syria. Disorder and disruption continued, while the defensive strength of the land diminished. Jews and Christians alike were increasingly persecuted. While their subjects' interests were neglected, the Fatimid rulers grew wealthier. Possibly the richest and certainly the cruelest of them was the Egyptian caliph al-Hakim, who ruled from 996 to 1021 C.E. He called himself the selected representative of God on earth and persecuted those who questioned his divinity no matter what their religion.

In 1009 C.E., Hakim ordered the destruction of Jewish and Christian houses of worship in his realm. The Church of the Holy Sepulchre was almost entirely destroyed, but not until after its wealth had been seized for the caliph. To save themselves from being slaughtered, thousands of Jews and Christians converted to Islam, or pretended to. Hakim decreed also, in 1010 C.E., that unconverted Jews must wear bells on their clothing and six-pound wooden blocks about their necks to show everyone they were stubborn unbelievers.

Hakim's death at age thirty-six remains a mystery. Some say he simply disappeared; others that his subjects rebelled and he was at last executed by order of his own sister. His memory is still at work, however. The *Druze*, a well-known Islamic sect in Israel and neighbor countries, still revere Hakim as he wished to be revered when he lived.

The name *Druze* comes from Dorazi, the name of the sect's founder. The 150,000 Druze now living are divided among Israel, southern Syria, and Lebanon. During the Six-Day War of June 1967 the Druze of Israel fought bravely for that country. Those from Syria and Lebanon served on the Arab side, however.

Continuing conflicts between rival Moslem rulers and regimes within and around Palestine and Syria provided opportunities that excited the territorial ambitions of the Greek Orthodox monarchs of the Byzantine empire to the north. They sent their warriors southward and made important inroads into the territory under Moslem rule, taking Antioch, Aleppo, and the island of Cyprus, and finally invading Palestine itself during the latter half of the tenth century. The Byzantines captured centers even as far south as the coastal city of Caesarea.

With such a start, the Byzantine leaders began to think and talk in terms of a still more significant prize: the hill-girt sacred city of Jerusalem itself. They cloaked that hope, however, in pious rhetoric. They wished to take, or "liberate," Jerusalem— "for the sake of Christianity." It was a Byzantine emperor, Johannes Tzimisces, ruler for some eight years beginning in 969, who told of his burning desire to pray at Jerusalem's Church of the Holy Sepulchre and to walk in the footsteps of Jesus, his Christ—especially mentioning Nazareth in the Galilee, and Mount Tabor. He could do so only—and this seemed clear—if those sacred sites were wrested from the hands of the Moslem "unbelievers."

Thus was sounded a threatening note that was to reecho, with loud and bloody clangor, later on, when the Crusades were being preached and organized in Europe, far to the north and west of the Greek Orthodox Byzantine empire.

Accompanying the pious aspirations of the Byzantine emperor and others were the commercial interests of powerful Italian merchants, especially those in Venice. Commerce had been growing between Europe and the land today called Israel. The merchants wanted for themselves a larger share in this trade. Also, there had come about a sizable increase in the number of European pilgrimages to the Holy Land—the tourist trade of that time. In the eleventh century, in fact, as many as twelve thousand pilgrims at a time were said to have visited Palestine. Travelers in such numbers had to be transported, guided, fed, and housed. All this meant possible profits, of which the Italian merchant-princes could never get enough.

This important pilgrimage "trade" was self-stimulating. Pilgrims, after they returned to Europe, spoke with fervor of the feelings of sanctity and inner benefit they had experienced during their unforgettable sojourn in the land where Jesus himself had trod.

The Fatimid dynasty, which held Jerusalem and the other principal holy sites, made some concessions to the wishes of the great but unwieldy Byzantine empire. In return for the release of some Moslem prisoners held by the Byzantines, permission was given for the rebuilding of the Church of the Holy Sepulchre. Also, funds from Byzantine (Greek Orthodox) coffers paid for the renovation of other churches, making the Holy Land even more of a magnet for pilgrims.

Early in the eleventh century another link was added to the lengthening chain of Moslem dynasties that one after another held sway over Jerusalem and its surrounding territory. This time the Fatimid dynasty gave way to the first Turkish Moslem rulers, the *Seljuks.*

Seljuk was a Turkish chieftain. After he and his people adopted the religion of Islam they became known as "the Seljuk Turks." Like other Turkish tribes, they supplied the fierce mercenaries on whom the older Islamic dynasties more and more depended to do their fighting for them.

Seljuk's grandson, Toghrul Beg, won important victories in wars in Persia and elsewhere on behalf of the Fatimid rulers. He could not long be denied the prize of the highest power for himself. By 1055 he had made himself *sultan,* meaning "master." The old line of Fatimids who had supplied the caliphs were assigned to deal with minor matters of religion. Now the control of ruling and fighting was in the hands of the new Turkish master and the line of sultans that followed him.

The Seljuk sultans, famed as fierce and tough fighters, soon brought under their unified rule large parts of the East. By 1070 C.E. they were in Syria, and before 1071 their general Atsiz had led his forces into Palestine. They took Ramla and without much trouble captured Jerusalem from its Fatimid defenders. The rest of Palestine, save for the coastal area and its fortress at Ashkelon, also fell before them.

During 1071 the Seljuk fighters continued northward, defeating the Byzantine forces in Armenia and threatening Constantinople itself.

The Christian pilgrims in Jerusalem were shocked and outraged by the new Seljuk policies. They were charged heavy fees, insulted, and generally mistreated. The terror-struck Byzantines set aside old animosities and sent a plea to the Roman Catholic pope and to the entire western world. In effect they pictured themselves as the eastern outpost of world Christianity, now in imminent danger of being wiped out by the infidel Turks.

Atsiz, the Seljuk warlord, was campaigning against Egypt when he was recalled to deal with a revolt in Jerusalem in 1076. Furious, he retook Jerusalem and ordered the slaughter of many of its inhabitants. Twenty years later, in 1096, the Fatimids were able to regain Jerusalem, this time without massacre or plunder of property. It was to be merely a brief interlude, however, for three years later, on July 15, 1099, Jerusalem was taken again, for the fourth time in less than thirty years. In this conquest, the bloodiest and most barbaric of all, the victors had come from Europe. They were the Crusaders, who for a significant period made themselves the feudal masters of the land.

12

THE BLOODY ERA
OF THE
CRUSADERS

(TO ABOUT 1300)

If only you would destroy the wicked, O God,
and the men of blood were to depart from me!

Wickedly they invoke your name;
[they] swear faithless oaths.

—FROM PSALM 139

The land we know as Israel was the goal of the Crusades, a strange and shockingly brutal movement or series of movements from Europe. The ostensible reason for the Crusades was the outrage felt by European Christians at the Turkish destruction of Christian shrines and the persecution of Christian pilgrims. "Save the sacred places from the infidel!" was the call that recruited many pious Christians.

Behind this religious mask, however, hard economic motives were at work. The Roman Catholic Church, centered at Rome, jealous of the hold of its rival, the Greek Orthodox Church, over Byzantium and the eastern countries, wished to establish its own foothold there. Merchants and shipowners, especially those in Italian ports, coveted a larger share in the increasingly rich commerce with Moslem countries.

Christian traders in Arab lands were continually harassed by Moslem bandits. The rigid old Byzantine empire, weakened by disunity, could not seem to provide protection for the profit-hungry Christian merchants.

Within Europe itself, under the feudal system prevalent there, conflict also prevailed. Nobles fought nobles; nobles fought their kings; princes of the Church were often princes of the land too, with very worldly ambitions. The campaign for the Crusades provided a way to unite the warring powers of Roman Catholic lands against the Turks, a common outside foe, and in so doing to win many advantages.

Pope Urban II was the principal, though not the only, propa-

[151]

gandist for the First Crusade. To its banner flocked people of all kinds and from all parts of Europe—knights, nobles, adventurers, criminals, freed slaves and prisoners, merchants, rascals, vagrants, priests, monks, hermits, and more.

As they journeyed by foot and horse to free the Holy Land from the infidel, they left through Europe a trail of terror, plunder, robbery, rape, and murder. Their principal victims were the Jews. The pope had assured those who joined the Crusade that their sins would be forgiven. No deed therefore seemed too dark.

There were, in all, eight different Crusades during a period extending for almost two centuries. Some Crusaders reached Palestine; others died or were diverted on the way. The toll in deaths from disease, hunger, and violence en route was staggering. This book tells only of the Crusades as they touched the land known as Israel. Touch it they did—with sound and fury, and with indelibly bloody marks.

The First Crusade was in its third year in June of 1099 when a force of some twelve thousand surviving Crusaders, having occupied Jaffa and Ramla, at last stood before the walls of Jerusalem itself. They lifted their calloused hands to heaven, removed their dusty shoes, and bent down to kiss the sacred soil. They too were stirred by the sight of the holy city.

Only one thousand Fatimid troops were on hand to defend Jerusalem. They tried to negotiate, seeking a peaceful settlement with the Franks. ("Franks" was the name then used in the Middle East for people who came from either what is now western Germany or northern France. The modern name of France, in fact, is derived from the earlier name "Frank.") The Fatimid commander of Jerusalem offered to guarantee that Christian pilgrims would be safe and well treated in that city. But none of his pleas had any effect. The leaders of the Crusade demanded nothing less than unconditional surrender.

After weeks of harrowing siege, the city was taken. A massacre followed that has never been forgotten throughout the Moslem world. Almost forty thousand inhabitants of Jerusalem were slaughtered: men and women, children and old people, soldiers, Moslems and Jews. Many were tortured, then burned to death. Some were shot with arrows, others were thrown from the walls or forced to jump from towers.

The Jews of Jerusalem who helped the Fatimid soldiers in their vain defense were forced into their synagogue and burned alive. Streets were piled with corpses and strewn with severed arms, hands, legs, and heads.

Then the conquering Crusaders strode through those bloodied streets to the Church of the Holy Sepulchre, where they gave thanks to Jesus "with weeping and rejoicing."

To the territory they had thus conquered in Palestine they gave the name "Kingdom of Jerusalem" and eventually crowned one of their leaders as its king. The word *Latin* was added later—Latin Kingdom of Jerusalem. This emphasized that it was the *Roman* Catholic religion that now held sway, not the *Greek* Orthodox. The new rulers soon expanded their control considerably: from Beirut, Lebanon, in the north, through the Negev wilderness to Eilat at the southern tip; and west to Egypt.

These Europeans, or "Franks," ruled Jerusalem and much more for an eighty-eight-year period, and then for about an additional one hundred years they remained in control of some parts of the land that became Israel. The era of the Crusades was a time of nearly total extinction of Jewish life in that land. In relation to the number of surviving Jews, the brutalities of the feudal Crusader rulers exceeded the worst that the Romans had committed. A complete feudal system was imposed on the land, and it operated more rigidly even than at home in Europe.

The few surviving Jews desperately sought to find some way to exist. At first the old ban against Jews living in Jerusalem was revived, save for a few families with special permission from the ruler of the Kingdom of Jerusalem.

In Europe itself, life for Jews had worsened. Thousands had been robbed, injured, or killed outright by the Crusaders on their way south. Darkness seemed to be engulfing Jews everywhere.

Such Jewish community life as did continue in Israel under the Franks was largely centered in Acre. In the year 1167 the great Moses Maimonides visited there and found about two hundred

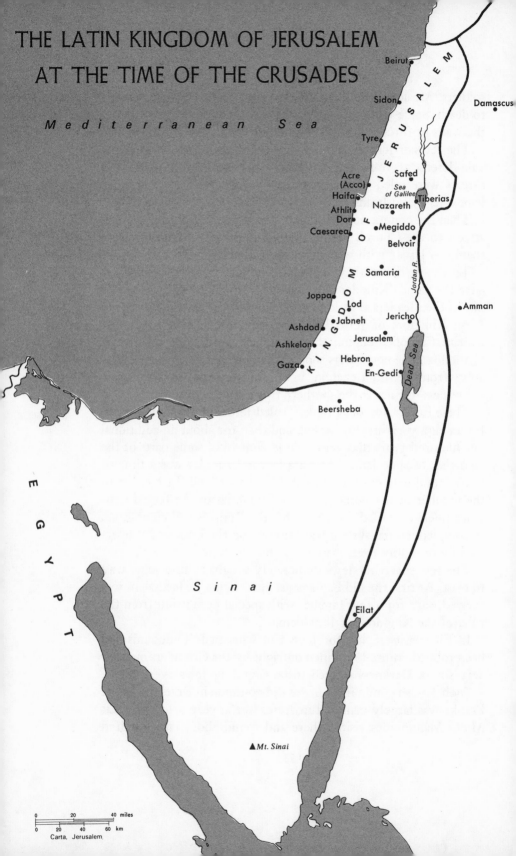

THE LATIN KINGDOM OF JERUSALEM
AT THE TIME OF THE CRUSADES

Mediterranean   Sea

Beirut

Sidon

Damascus

Tyre

Acre
(Acco)   Safed
Haifa   *Sea
of Galilee*
Athlit   Nazareth   Tiberias
Dor
Caesarea   Megiddo

Belvoir

Samaria

Joppa
Lod
Jabneh   Jericho
Ashdod
Ashkelon   Jerusalem
Gaza   Hebron
En-Gedi

Dead Sea

Amman

Jordan R.

Beersheba

E
G
Y
P
T

S i n a i

Eilat

▲*Mt. Sinai*

0   20   40 miles
0   20   40   60 km
Carta, Jerusalem.

Jewish families. During the year 1211 three hundred rabbis and scholars, fleeing from persecution in England and France, reached Acre. However, Talmudic studies dwindled throughout Palestine.

During the time of the Latin Kingship a constant stream of European feudal nobles and men-at-arms arrived in the country and set themselves up, or tried to, as feudal lords on parcels of land assigned to them by their overlords. Members of the Moslem population, or even Greek Orthodox Christians, who had lived there and in many cases had been the previous owners of the land were now used as serfs by the Crusader lords. As usual in feudalism, there were two separate sets of laws: one for the landed nobles, another for the common city citizens. And for the serfs there was very little in the way of justice. Their welfare was left to the whims of their overlords.

Pilgrimages from Europe became big business during the era of the "Latin" Crusaders. Two separate and rival organizations competed for this trade—the Knights of the Temple, or Templars, and the Hospitalers. Both had been established by the Crusaders in Jerusalem, supposedly to provide protection and care for pilgrims. Both made rich profits from their hostels, their sales of holy relics and souvenirs, and their land acquisitions. They became wealthy, corrupt, and dissolute.

Gradually Jews were allowed to come back to Jerusalem again. There, as in other parts of the land at this time, they were occupied chiefly as dyers and glassmakers, but they had to pay the Christian Crusader king for the right to work at these skilled trades. Both Jews and "Syrians," as the native-born Christians were called by the Franks, were restricted to that part of the old walled city of Jerusalem now known as the Moslem quarter. The city at that time was a strange mixture of European and eastern Christians, of Armenians, Arabs, and various other groups and sects. It was a time of much interbreeding.

It has been written that in about 1169 Jews were for a short time expelled from the city. However, an eminent Jewish traveler, Benjamin of Tudela, visited Jerusalem about that time and reported that there were some two hundred Jews living in a corner "under the Tower of David," a structure today called the Citadel.

Many attempts were made by the Moslems to regain their lost territory in Palestine. Success came only in the days of the remarkable ruler known as Saladin (Salah-ed-Din-Yusuf, 1138-1193).

Saladin was an intelligent, liberal-minded Moslem prince who in 1171 had defeated the last of the Fatimid line of caliphs and brought Egypt and Syria under his control, thus establishing the Ayyubid dynasty. By 1184 with energy and careful planning he had begun a campaign to drive out the Crusaders. For this anti-Crusader crusade he mobilized 100,000 fighters.

He scored a great victory in July 1187 at Hattin north of Lake Tiberias. The Crusader king, Guy of Lusignan, was taken prisoner. Then Saladin went on to capture more than a dozen well-fortified Crusader-held towns, including Acre, from which he set free four thousand imprisoned Moslems.

Factional strife had rent the Latin Kingdom. Jerusalem, whose Christian forces had declined, had become vulnerable to attack. Saladin reached its walls in late September 1187 and offered the Christian commanders safety for their lives and property if they would surrender without struggle. They refused. Within a few weeks Saladin's men had captured the city.

This time there was no massacre. Saladin turned a deaf ear to fellow-Moslems who urged revenge for the bloodbath that had taken place eighty-eight years earlier. He spared the lives of the sixty thousand inhabitants, setting free the poor but demanding ransom in gold from the rich. About fifteen thousand unransomed Christians became slaves.

Saladin showed himself friendly to the few remaining Jews of Jerusalem. This has been attributed to the influence of his own court physician, the brilliant scholar and man of medicine Moses Maimonides. Saladin allowed Jews to return to Jerusalem to live, to labor, to pray and to mourn. There they have remained ever since. During one significant interval, 1948-1967, Jews were excluded from the Old City of Jerusalem, including the Temple site and the Western Wall when it was held by Jordan. But even then, not far away beyond barbed-wire barriers, Jews lived and labored in sections of Jerusalem farther west.

The retaking of Jerusalem by Moslems appalled most European Christians. The feudal Crusader lords now retained only three cities in the East.

But a Third Crusade was soon under way. Its goal was to win back the tomb of Christ—and also the feudal lands of the Frankish lords. Its leaders were drawn from Europe's top royalty: Richard the Lionhearted, king of England, and the young Philip Augustus, king of France. These new Crusaders did take Acre in 1191. Then the French king, ill, returned to his native land. And Richard went on to battle Saladin for Jerusalem itself.

Besides his "lion heart," Richard was equipped with a fairly good military mind. He soon saw that it was no use trying to defeat these determined Moslems in their own land, where the climate seemed to assist them and to hinder the northerners. Saladin, too, wisely realized that the increasingly powerful Christians of the West could not be kept always from their holiest shrines.

The two leaders got together and arranged a three-year truce. Jerusalem, they agreed, would continue under Moslem rule, but Christians would be allowed to visit their shrines without paying any fees. The Crusaders, for their part, would keep control of the coast between Acre and Jaffa, an arrangement that would continue to benefit the Italian merchants, who had profited from the existence of the Frankish kingdom. Both Moslems and Christians were to be allowed to pass freely into and through the territory of the "other side," so long as they did so in a peaceful, friendly manner.

Saladin died in 1193, after which his considerable empire began to break up. A Sixth Crusade was launched, bringing to the Holy Land the young "Holy Roman Emperor" Frederick II, ruler, in fact, of the unlikely combination of Germany and Sicily. He found when he arrived that he was given the cold shoulder by the Christians of the coastal region. He had previously declined to join an earlier Crusade, for which sin he had been excommunicated by the pope in Rome.

Frederick followed the pattern provided by Richard before

him. He got together with the Moslem ruler, now el Kamil, the new sultan of Egypt and Syria Palestine. To the surprise of the world, they signed a treaty in 1229. It gave Frederick control of most of Jerusalem as well as of Bethlehem, Nazareth, Sidon, Acre, and Jaffa. The Moslems, for their part, were to have control of the top of Mount Moriah in Jerusalem, which gave them their own Dome of the Rock on the Haram, where the last Jewish Temple had stood.

The pope in Rome was outraged. He refused to recognize this pact, calling it an insult to Christianity—in effect, a "sellout." Once Frederick had left the region, Christian leaders who remained took control of all Jerusalem and aligned themselves with a rival Moslem group in Damascus. The sultan of Egypt, threatened by this new combination, called for help from an independent Turkish tribe, the Kwarizmians, who had moved into Syria and Palestine from Persia, which they had left when fleeing from Genghis Khan's invaders from faraway Mongolia. Thus invited, the Kwarizmian Turks quickly occupied Jerusalem and went on a rampage of plunder and massacre in which large numbers of the city's inhabitants were slain.

This savage interlude was brief. Soon Jerusalem was wrested from the run-amok Kwarizmians by an army sent from Egypt and composed primarily of Turkish slaves and servants who served as the shock troops of the Ayyubid rulers there. The military genius at the head of this strange slave army was a memorable figure, Baibars by name, himself also a slave in origin. In 1244 he first defeated the Crusaders at Gaza on the coast, then came inland and captured Jerusalem from the Kwarizmians.

In 1249, shortly afterward, these Turkish soldier-slaves became supreme masters in Egypt, after ousting the declining Ayyubid dynasty. The new dynasty, destined to endure for more than 250 years, became known in history as the *Mamelukes* or *Mamluks*, from a word meaning "owned" or "enslaved."

By 1260 Baibars himself had become the sultan in Egypt and thus ruler over its Palestinian territories. It was an era of incessant and almost intolerable conflict. The Mongols under Genghis Khan had thrust ever deeper into the Middle East.

THE BLOODY ERA OF THE CRUSADERS

Even after the great Genghis himself died in 1227, his successors in command continued westward, taking Bagdad in 1258 and Damascus in 1260. Baibars finally halted their long advance in a historic battle at Ein Harod about 25 miles south and west of the Sea of Galilee and barely 100 miles from modern Jerusalem's outskirts.

Thus Baibars drove the Mongols out of Palestine and then out of Syria also. It was their first decisive defeat in their long and devastating invasion, a stupendous procession of conquest that had carried them thousands of miles west of distant Mongolia. On the way they had so ravaged Mesopotamia that its agriculture and economy have never fully recovered to this day.

Jerusalem suffered terribly from this conflict, but indirectly, since the formidable Mongols did not actually enter the city.

In checking the Mongol threat, Baibars won for himself an eminent place in Moslem history—on a par with their other great leaders and monarchs. His greatest glory, in the eyes of most Moslems, was probably his victories over the Crusaders, whom he drove out of important positions in Palestine and even, before he died in 1277, from their stronghold in Antioch, Syria.

Baibars's successors in the Mameluke line continued relentlessly to rid the Middle East of the unwelcome European intruders. One by one, the remaining Crusader strongholds were taken: Acre, Beirut, Sidon, and Tyre. By 1291 the last of the Crusader feudal nobles and warlords had been ousted from the soil of the Middle East.

Once again Moslem control had become complete in all of what we now know as Israel, Jordan, Lebanon, and Syria. It remained so, with various changes of regimes and rulers, during the following more than six hundred years. In fact, that longtime Moslem mastery ended only in late 1917 during World War I. It was then that Turkish forces, allied with the Germans, were defeated by the British expeditionary forces operating under General Allenby in Palestine.

Though the Frankish or Crusader rulers and warriors were expelled before the end of the thirteenth century, their traces can still be found in the history-rich land of Israel—the remains of their towers, forts, walls, and other ruins. Their backward feudal system of ownership and rule notwithstanding, the Crusader monarchs and nobles did build bridges of communication between the Holy Land and Europe, which was becoming ever more dynamic and influential in the world. Despite their brutalities, their oppressions, and their greed, the Crusaders served as links in an important chain.

Never again, during all the centuries from the fourteenth to the twentieth, was the land that became Israel completely cut off for any long period from the trade, the close attention, and even the territorial ambitions of the rising powers in Europe. Nor, for that matter, from those later offshoots of the European powers—their "colonies," which after the end of the fifteenth century began to be implanted in the New World of North and South America.

13

MAMELUKES, MYSTICS, AND FALSE MESSIAHS

(TO ABOUT 1750)

With a loud voice I cry out to the Lord . . .
My complaint I pour out before him . . .
When my spirit is faint within me,
  you know my path.

In the way along which I walk
  they have laid a trap for me.
. . . I have lost all means of escape;
  there is no one who cares for my life.

Attend to my cry,
  for I am brought low indeed.
. . . Lead me forth from prison,
  that I may give thanks to your name.

—FROM PSALM 142

F ar-reaching changes, strife, and bitter warfare punctuated the
closing decades of the twelfth century and most of the
thirteenth in this troubled part of the world. The prevailing
situation as well as the prospects of the Jews in what is now
Israel reflected, with increasing emphasis, the many disruptions.

When the Mameluke dynasty began to rule in the middle
1240s, the population in their realm—notably in Egypt, North
Africa, Palestine, and Syria—was less than half of what it had
been less than a century before!

The comparative shrinkage in numbers was still greater in the
case of the Jews. This was all the more striking since it followed
a period, about half a century earlier, when Jews had been invited and even urged to return to live in Jerusalem and elsewhere. That period of welcome and promise had begun after
Saladin took Jerusalem. A rabbi who visited Palestine in 1216
stated that Saladin while alive had urged Jews to return there—
especially those who had fled to escape the terrors of the Crusader
rule.

Indeed, a Jewish community did begin to grow in Jerusalem.
It was divided into "congregations" or groups, according to
the part of the world from which their members had returned.
There were congregations of westerners (meaning mainly Europeans) and North Africans, among others. The westerners came
to include chiefly Jews who had arrived from Spain and
Germany.

Elsewhere in Palestine, also, signs of Jewish return and recovery appeared during this period of relative peace and promise. However, mainly because of the wars and disasters of the 1240s and 1250s, conditions again grew increasingly unfavorable.

By 1263, a traveler visiting the land reported that "only a handful" of Jews still existed there. The region as a whole was largely desolate; Jerusalem even more so. Its former Jewish residents had fled to the ancient and venerable city of Shechem, taking with them their precious Torah. In 1260 a Talmudic college or academy had been established at Acre on the coast, but only thanks to the support of Jewish communities in France and England. Acre, in fact, became the site of the leading remaining community of Jews in Palestine, far surpassing Jerusalem for many years.

These observations are underscored by the testimony of Rabbi Moses ben Nachmanides (1194–1270), a physician, theologian, and mystic. Having been driven out of Spain, he came to the Holy Land. There, in the 1260s, he found things in a deplorable state. Jerusalem, he discovered, was even worse off than many other parts of the country, most of which became the arena for the final conflict between the Crusaders and the Moslems. The rabbi reported that there lived—or existed—amidst the rubble of Jerusalem about two thousand Moslems and only three hundred Christians. As for Jews, he could find only one or two families, working as dyers.

Another visitor to Jerusalem in 1267 recorded that it was impossible to assemble there even the minimum number of ten men—the *minyon* or quorum—required to conduct Jewish worship.

Nevertheless, even then when Jewish residence in the city of the lost Temple had sunk almost to nothing, some Jewish pilgrims still managed to arrive for their holy days. The ancient tradition of "going up to Jerusalem" for the holidays survived in those dark times even as it had when the glorious Temple built by Herod still stood resplendent atop Mount Moriah.

During the fourteenth century, under the reign of Mameluke rulers, the Jewish population of the land of Israel gradually increased. This was true especially in the towns of Acre and Jerusalem. Ramla likewise was said to have some Jews, and a small Jewish community was established at Beth-shean.

By the second half of the fourteenth century most of the newly arriving Jewish settlers came from France or Germany. They worked in farming, in handicrafts, or as merchants. Before long, even some physicians and technicians were added to their number.

Catastrophes continued to make life hazardous and miserable for most. There were famines, droughts, earthquakes, and devastating epidemics. Palestine was struck by the "Black Death," the plague that had decimated the populations of Europe and Egypt around the middle of that century. Jews and other Palestinian residents died in great numbers. One unverified report spoke of twenty-two thousand deaths within a single week in the town of Gaza alone.

The exhausting wars which had driven out the Crusaders before the end of the thirteenth century left in their wake lingering woes: high taxes, high prices, and grinding, bitter poverty. Mameluke military expenditures drained their subjects. Mameluke bureaucrats and officials—even the governors of Palestine—quarreled and conspired against each other. The regime was corrupt and costly. Bedouins and bandits roamed the countryside, attacking and robbing settlements and travelers. In 1481 such marauders plundered and burned Ramla itself. Even Jerusalem was attacked and its governor forced to flee. Such miseries made the people long to be rid of their Mameluke rulers and helped make easier the eventual victory of the Ottomans early in the sixteenth century.

Nevertheless, as the fifteenth century neared its end, more and more Jews came to live in the land. Pilgrimages were on the increase. Europe was reading more and listening more to reports of travelers returned from the Holy Land. Felix Fabri, a Christian visiting Jerusalem in the early 1480s, told of 500 Jewish families living there. A Jewish traveler of about the same time reported only approximately half that many. But even that would have been a great increase over the days when it was not possible to bring together as many as ten adult male Jews to form the quorum required to worship the God of Israel.

Fabri's account is colorful and vivid. He found the hill-girt city of Jerusalem to be somewhat like Basle, Switzerland. He saw ruined houses being used as dumping places for dead animals. The holy city was certainly in a semi-ruined state. Its population was a mixture of people from nearly all the known world. Jews and Christians alike were poor and suffered from high taxes. Both, according to Christian travelers, were looked on by the Moslems as "no better than dogs."

Jewish travelers saw the same poverty and ruin. However, compared with the persecution and humiliation that most Jews were then undergoing in Europe, conditions in Israel seemed preferable to them.

Rabbi Meshullam ben Menahem was a 1481 visitor who found much to admire. Though it was desolate and partly in ruins, he found that this part of Palestine was fertile, a land of "milk and honey." It abounded, he reported, with honey of various kinds, with oil of olive and sesame, with wheat and barley grain, with pomegranates and other good fruits, all at prices that he considered low.

Regarding the eating habits of the people, "The Moslems and also the Jews of this place . . . eat out of one vessel with their fingers, without a napkin . . ." However, he hastened to add, "their clothes are clean."

As many times before and since, resident Jews of Jerusalem often earned their living as guides to the holy places. Others were peddlers, handworkers, or merchants. Relatively few were now active in farming, not only because of the crushing taxes but also because such work was looked on with contempt by the Moslem rulers. The main source of Jewish support and survival, however, continued to be contributions from Jews living in communities outside the land.

In this latter part of the fifteenth century both Jews and Christians were barred from the Temple mount and from the tomb of the patriarchs at Hebron. However, Jews did manage to get permission to build a synagogue on the slopes of David's Mount Zion near Mount Moriah. A Franciscan chapel, by this time in ruins, stood on the site of the intended synagogue. The monks of this order grew furious when they heard that a Jewish house of worship might be built there. They appealed to the pope in Rome, warning that if the Jews were allowed to do this, they would some day take over even the Church of the Holy Sepulchre itself.

As a countermeasure the pope issued an edict to the Venetian shipowners: No Jew could be transported to Palestine on a Christian-owned ship. Since the Venetians controlled nearly all Mediterranean shipping, Jews now found the water route closed to them.

The old, outworn, but still significant eastern Roman (Byzantine) empire suffered a fatal loss when, in 1453, the Ottoman Turks captured the famous city of Constantinople and made it their capital. Thus ended Byzantine rule—an empire of amazing duration. In its place arose Turkey, the empire of the Ottomans.*

Speedily the new Moslem Turkey opened its doors to Jews. In 1456, three years after the fall of Constantinople, a visitor to that country praised the honorable treatment of Jews by Turkey and urged Jews to settle there, pointing out that from Turkey they could now reach Palestine by land. Thousands of Jews took his advice. Many used Turkey as a way station, traveling on to Palestine from there. But great numbers stayed on in Turkey and became citizens. Soon Constantinople had a Jewish community of about thirty thousand—larger than any other in all Europe. There were forty-four synagogues. In general these Jews seem to have led lives of security and self-respect. Many attained positions of importance and profit in professions and in public life. But Palestine still lured others.

For about fifteen hundred years, beginning in days of the old Roman empire, Jews had lived continuously in Spain and

---

* The name *Ottoman* comes from Osman, 1259 to 1326 C.E., founder of this formidable regime. It had started as a small fighting tribe of Moslem Turks who had fled from the Mongol advance and settled in Asia. Swiftly they expanded their control until they ruled all the lands bordering the eastern Mediterranean. They were responsible for making Turkey a power even in Europe.

Portugal. But on March 31, 1492, under an infamous edict of the Christian rulers, all Jews who refused to convert to Christianity were expelled from Spain. In 1496 Portugal issued a similar law. The ships of Columbus, setting out for the New World, passed vessels in the harbors of Spain loaded with desperate Jewish refugees. Many of these settled in Turkey, others in the Holy Land.

By the end of the fifteenth century, Jews had been forcibly ousted from almost all of western Europe except Germany and Italy. Many fled to Poland, others to the southeastern countries under Moslem rule.

To these Jews in search of survival the attitudes of the Ottoman rulers of Turkey became especially important, for now they were the masters of Palestine.

In 1517, when the Ottomans drove the despised Mameluke rulers out of Palestine, that land's population had been considerably reduced and those who remained were poverty-stricken. The next four centuries under Ottoman rule brought important changes. Once again the little land became a link between two major populated regions: the Ottoman capital, Constantinople, to the north, and Egypt and North Africa to the southwest.

The Ottomans joined Palestine to Syria and strengthened the defenses of the merged provinces. They tried, not always successfully, to protect pilgrims visiting the sacred places. Bedouins and Druze tribesmen, and even the peasantry (called *fellahin*), harassed the travelers, attacking, robbing and even killing them.

These problems were intensified by the almost constant warfare of the Ottoman Turks against European countries to the west and Persia to the east. By the last quarter of the sixteenth century, internal rebellions of Moslem subjects of the Turks had become so severe that farming, industry, and commerce were almost at a standstill. In large areas tax collections stopped.

At the summit of the regime, however, there was wealth and even splendor under the greatest of the Ottoman rulers, Suleiman the Magnificent, 1520 to 1566 C.E. He was an enthusiastic builder and spent large sums of money on the restoration and erection of Islamic shrines in Palestine. During his reign the damaged old walls of Jerusalem were rebuilt and given imposing gates.

Fountains were provided in the city; atop Mount Moriah the sacred Haram platform was renewed, and the lovely Dome of the Rock was resplendent with a new glazed tile exterior. Even in modern Jerusalem many evidences of Suleiman's magnificence and munificence can be seen.

When the Ottoman rule began, the total Jewish population, by one estimate, was only some five hundred families; one-third to one-half of these were located in Jerusalem itself. However, by the midpoint of the sixteenth century the total number of residents of Palestine was about three hundred thousand, 90 percent of them Moslem. Of the thirty thousand non-Moslems, Jews probably constituted a substantial share, though it is not possible to estimate precisely how many.

The Jewish population of Jerusalem itself is better known. In this period about one thousand Jews, three thousand Christians, and six thousand Moslems lived there—a mere ten thousand in all. And there were Jewish communities in Tiberias, Acre, Gaza, and Hebron.

The Jews then living in Israel enjoyed freedom of worship and were permitted to administer their own marriage, divorce, and inheritance laws. However, they had little or no share in the government or the political life of the land as a whole.

Safed, a colorful hill city in the Galilee, became for a significant period the center of Jewish spiritual life. It was said to contain more than a thousand Jewish families, thus exceeding the Jewish population of Jerusalem. It was also a center for a growing textile and cloth-dyeing industry and a transit point and market for farm products en route to Damascus in what is now Syria.

Safed's commercial importance and wealth declined somewhat after the Turks occupied the island of Cyprus in 1571 and forced some of the Safed citizens to move to Cyprus in order to help develop the island's economy.

However, Safed's greatest significance was not in fabrics, dyestuffs, or farm produce, for it became a unique center of Jewish religious study and scholarship. Scholars and rabbis had come there from Spain, Portugal, Sicily, and elsewhere. During the

[169]

sixteenth century, Jacob Berab even tried to set up at Safed a Sanhedrin, on the old model, to govern religious affairs for all Jewry. The attempt failed, largely because by this time the Jews, so widely scattered in the world, were too divided as to language, habits, and way of life.

Safed did become the great center for Jewish mysticism— for the esoteric studies of the Cabbala, and for various messianic prophecies and superstitions. The pressures of sorrow over past losses and the fears of new persecutions in the future impelled Jewish thinkers toward mysticism. They sought escape in symbolic, numerologic, and even half-magical speculations. The sages of Safed were driven inward by the bitter blows of the real world. They sought a better world, but along paths far removed from grim reality.

In the sixteenth century Safed served as sanctuary for, among others, Rabbi Isaac Luria (1534–1572), a noted mystic and cabbalist. Another famous resident was Rabbi Joseph Caro (1488–1575), author of the *Shulhan Arukh*, meaning "prepared table," a four-volume popular summary of the Talmud. Its tabulations offered guidance for every aspect of daily conduct for orthodox Jews. It was used widely for centuries after Caro's death and is still referred to.

In 1563 the first printing press in the entire Ottoman empire was set up at Safed. Books printed there in Hebrew and sent far and wide were prized not only in Israel but throughout the world. The 1565 edition of Caro's *Shulhan Arukh* was one of the first publications from this press.

Today Safed is a major attraction for visitors. For many religious Jews its greatest appeal lies in its old synagogues and in the tales about its vanished scholars, mystics, and cabbalists. For tourists in general it is an attractive and intriguing art colony.

The sixteenth century was also the period of Joseph Nasi, a wealthy and influential Jew born in Portugal. He rose high in Turkish governmental circles, becoming advisor to the great sultan Suleiman the Magnificent.

Like Theodor Herzl in nineteenth-century Europe, Nasi was

concerned for the fate of Jewish refugees from persecution. He conceived the idea of a resettlement plan to help them. Suleiman and his son, Prince Selim II, supported Nasi and deeded to him the city of Tiberias, plus a region around it with some seven villages, to serve as a homeland for refugee Jews. Nasi hoped to make of Tiberias a silk manufacturing center to compete with the silk trade of Venice. Mulberry trees were planted, silkworms and silk-weaving looms imported. For the manufacture of cloth and clothing, Nasi also got wool from Spain.

The first shiploads of Jewish immigrants who sailed from Italy bound for this Tiberias colony were captured by pirates from Malta and sold as slaves. The new colony did at last make a start, but it collapsed when Nasi lost interest and failed to provide it with the necessary support.

Jews of Israel were engaged now mainly in the clothing trades, textile making and dyeing, and shoemaking. In addition to those who managed to be self-supporting, there were many rabbis, scholars, and students, the sick, aged, and destitute, whose existence was made possible only by constant contributions from Jewish communities far from Israel.

Long centuries of living outside Israel had created two great groupings among Jews. Those who lived in the Iberian peninsula (Spain and Portugal), and who went from there to North Africa, came to be known as *Sephardim*, or *Sepharadim* in Hebrew. Those in the nations of northern Europe, and especially in Germany, Poland, and Russia, were called the *Ashkenazim*. Between the two groups there were distinct differences in language, speech, traditions, and habits. Some of these differences remain even today. Each group had its own synagogues, rabbis, schools, and charitable institutions. Usually the chief rabbi of Jerusalem was of Sephardic background. Today, since the establishment of the state of Israel in 1948, the Sephardic population has grown considerably, especially with the arrival of Jews from North Africa, Morocco, and Iran.

In spite of external differences, Sephardim and Ashkenazim shared one lamentable experience: both underwent brutal and savage persecution in their respective parts of the world. The middle of the seventeenth century brought to the Ashkenazi Jews living in Poland a terrible tragedy; the Ukrainian Cossacks under Bogdan Chmielnicki rebelled against the Polish nobles and the Catholic priests, then vented their rage against the Jews. Seven hundred Jewish communities in Poland were wiped out entirely and hundreds of thousands of Jews tortured and massacred.

Jews all over the world reacted with horror and sympathy. Funds that otherwise would have been sent to their co-religionists in Palestine were sent instead to Poland. With this money, thousands of Jews who had been sold into slavery, which at that time still existed there, were ransomed and released. (That rescue effort was more successful than the comparable effort when Nazi Germany was exterminating Jews. Leaders of Jewish organizations unsuccessfully tried to ransom the Jewish victims of the Hitler regime, which systematically slaughtered some five to six million Jews of all ages, along with lesser numbers of other ethnic groups, in the many Nazi extermination centers set up for the purpose.)

Most of the Jews of Palestine were reduced to bitter poverty as funds were diverted to aid the victims of the Polish massacres. Many Jews in Palestine died of disease and hunger, especially since during the latter half of the seventeenth century the Turkish governors imposed even heavier taxes and fines.

Desperation grew among Jews in Palestine and elsewhere in the world. As in earlier periods when things seemed intolerable, they longed for the appearance of a divinely sent redeemer or Messiah who would release them from their living nightmare. A mood of excitement grew, for it seemed conditions had become so bad that the end of the world could not be far distant. Many deeply religious Jews in Poland and elsewhere packed their most precious belongings and impatiently awaited the summons that they felt sure must come to take them back to their "land of promise," for only there, on the sacred soil itself, could the longed-for Messiah appear.

Self-proclaimed messiahs and prophets did appear. One of the most notorious of these, Shabbathai Zvi, arrived in Jerusalem soon after the middle of the seventeenth century. The council of rabbis there at first rejected and excommunicated him, but he was able to win over the leaders of the Jewish community after he had somehow extracted from the Turkish governing officials some concessions for them.

Eventually he went to Constantinople, the capital itself, for the announced purpose of demanding that the Turkish government give Palestine to the Jews. Instead, the sultan gave him the choice of converting to Islam or being put to death. When Shabbathai Zvi speedily chose to become a Moslem, most of his followers were plunged from their previous state of intoxication and antic-ipation into the depths of horror and humiliation. Some of them, however, followed him into Islam and formed the sect called *Dönmeh*, which venerated him. It persisted until the twentieth century.

During the period that followed Shabbathai Zvi, Jews more and more immersed themselves in mysticism and cabbalism, with-drawing from the world of reality to wrap their religious dreams about them like a cocoon. Increasingly they felt driven from the non-Jewish world in which their hopes and their humanity had for centuries been betrayed and mocked. Their horizons nar-rowed as they plumbed even deeper the depths within their sacred books and the imaginings of their own minds.

14

REVIVAL OF
AN ANCIENT DREAM

(TO ABOUT 1913)

Mighty is he! Mighty is he!
May he build his Temple soon.
Speedily, speedily,
In our lifetime let it be.
Build, O Lord! Build, O Lord!
Build your Temple speedily.

Righteous, perfect, one is he!
May he build his Temple soon.
Speedily, speedily,
In our lifetime let it be.

—from *Addir hu*, author unknown.
A traditional song, appealing for early
restoration of Zion, symbolized by the Temple.

During the eighteenth century the Ottoman empire began to disintegrate. Corruption and rivalries weakened it from within; warfare with Russia and threats from other nations of Europe pressured it from without. In stark contrast to its glories under Suleiman the Magnificent, the Ottoman regime, short of funds, became feeble and ineffective. Meanwhile, the great powers of Europe, especially Britain, France, and Russia, grew stronger, more imperialistic, and more demanding.

Within Palestine, rival local Moslem leaders engaged in endless disruptive feuds. Meanwhile, its Jewish population increased. Most of the new arrivals were a very special group of Ashkenazi Jews—members of the new *Hasidic* sect that had arisen in eastern Europe.

These Hasidim became important to the future of Israel. Their founder, Israel of Moldavia (1700–1760), was better known by his affectionate Hebrew title, *Baal Shem Tov*, meaning "Master of the Good Name."

The Baal Shem introduced a warmer, happier, more nourishing kind of Judaism than the gloomy, restrictive religious attitudes that were prevalent at the time. Rather than concentrating on legalistic hairsplitting of the rules and regulations for conduct, the Hasidim found joy in their sheer love of God and maintained a buoyant optimism despite all that the world might do to them. They took to song and dance as a suitable extension of their worship.

After the Baal Shem died his teachings were often diluted or distorted. Even during his life they had been denounced by the more formal and conventional rabbis. But the Baal Shem and his Hasidic followers did bring light into dark places and forced a reexamination or relaxation of hidebound habits in the daily religion of Jews.

Tiberias in Palestine had lain neglected and in ruins since the failure of the resettlement project launched there by Joseph Nasi. Now it was rebuilt by the Moslem governor of northern Palestine, who wished to enlarge the base from which he could collect taxes. He invited two Jewish families to move there from Damascus. By 1738 they had been joined by several more family groups, including merchants and bankers who helped develop the town and its environs.

Tiberias soon became a new Jewish center in the Galilee second in importance only to Safed itself. Safed, in fact, declined somewhat during that century, for it was struck by a plague in 1742 and an earthquake in 1769. But in 1776, the very year that the united colonies in North America declared their independence from Britain, Hasidim arriving from Russia increased again the numbers of Jews in Safed.

By the middle of the eighteenth century there were probably no more than three million Jews in all the world. Most of them lived in eastern Europe, to which their ancestors had fled during the Crusades after being uprooted from their old homes in the German Rhineland and elsewhere to the west. The Jewish population of Poland in the last half of the eighteenth century is estimated to have been about one and a half million, or half the world's total of Jews.

Other active Jewish communities existed also in Russia, Rumania, Austria, Prussia, Holland, France, Italy, and England; likewise in Africa, in Asia (under the Turkish empire), and as far away as China to the far east. Small groups of Jews were living even in North and South America, to the far west.

In 1759, in fact, a fund-raiser—a rabbi from the town of Safed —for the first time visited the British colonies (which were not yet the United States). In 1779, some three years after the Declaration of Independence, another fund-raiser from Israel was on hand. While in the young United States, he even helped with the Hebrew grammar of a prayer being composed in order that a Jewish congregation might pray for the well-being of the new American government. It was a small but significant gesture from one of the world's oldest peoples to the youngest nation.

The last decade of the eighteenth century brought drastic change, and fear of further change, to the established order in Europe. The French revolution unseated and then executed the king of France. By 1798 a brilliant, ambitious, and ruthless young French general, Napoleon Bonaparte, seeking to cut through Britain's route to its great colony of India, led an expedition into Egypt. He defeated the army of the Mamelukes who administered Egypt for the Ottoman Turks.

This French military success in Egypt was a serious setback for the Turks. Though their power had been dwindling in Egypt, they considered that country an important part of their empire. Now they allied themselves with the British against the French.

Napoleon, then only thirty, had another dream—to gain control of the ports of the eastern Mediterranean and create a link between Africa and India by conquering Palestine Syria, or Syria Palestine, as it was commonly called under the Turkish administration.

Early in 1799, Napoleon invaded Syria Palestine from the south. It was the first armed entry by Europeans since the Crusades. Napoleon led his small force of twelve thousand French troops northward, opposite to the direction of the thrusts earlier made by Alexander the Great and by the Crusaders on their way to take Jerusalem.

The French first took El-Arish, later to return to the spotlight of world attention during the Israeli Six-Day War in June 1967, about 168 years later. The invaders next captured Gaza, whose Jewish population fled before them. Then Napoleon led his men in the taking of Lod, Ramla, Jaffa, and the then small village of Haifa.

It was at Jaffa, today a suburb of the metropolis of Tel-Aviv, that the French encountered heavy resistance. After the city had been taken, General Bonaparte, with shocking brutality, ordered two thousand helpless Turkish prisoners executed in cold blood on the shore of the Mediterranean.

Napoleon himself never took time to visit Jerusalem. News of his advance, however, was carried to that city, and tales of his cruelty, especially to Jews, were spread by Turkish authorities. Feverish preparations to strengthen the city's defenses were made, many Jews taking part in these efforts, which were encouraged by one of their rabbis, Mordecai Joseph Meyuhas.

During his campaign in Syria Palestine, Napoleon confidently proclaimed to the Jews of the world that he would return to them their inheritance, meaning the land of Israel. During his later conquests in northern Europe, including the German Rhineland, he freed the Jews living there from their ghettoes. To many European Jews, thus freed from the irksome old restrictions and limitations, Napoleon seemed like a great liberator. Yet history shows that his actions with respect to the Jewish people were inconsistent: sometimes helpful, sometimes hostile, depending on what he believed, at the moment, would best advance his own ambitions. Early in the nineteenth century, after important military successes in Europe, he made what seemed at first a helpful proposal—to set up in France a Jewish Sanhedrin, or council, like that in Judea in the days of the Temple. No doubt he thought at the time that it might help him win the support of Jews in countries he would later seek to conquer. Such a Napoleon-sponsored body of Jews did meet as a Sanhedrin in France in 1807, but it died because of inactivity and loss of interest by Napoleon. A year later he issued a series of restrictive decrees directed against French Jews which remained in force for some ten years.

Napoleon's 1799 promise of their old homeland to the Jews of the world no doubt was based on his hope that it would rally for him Jewish military support in Syria Palestine, Africa, and Asia, and his further hope that Jews might help him to develop Israel after he had conquered it. Those Jews, however, did not go over to Napoleon. Many fought alongside the Arabs in defense of the land that was sacred to them all. It was easy for Jews living there to recall that the Turkish government, despite its shortcomings, had been more friendly to Jews than any Christian regime.

When Napoleon's forces reached the strongly fortified city of Acre, they met unusually heavy resistance from Turks, Arabs, and the supporting British fleet. Napoleon's two-month-long siege of that city failed. His loss of some three thousand men, plus an outbreak of the plague, forced him to give up his effort to conquer the land. He returned first to Egypt, and then to France.

He had expected that the disunited Moslem population and also the Christians in Palestine would give him essential aid. The Moslems, however, proved unwilling to join with French Christians "against their sultan," and the Christians played it safe, waiting to see whether the Turks or the French would win. Once Napoleon had returned to France, all Egypt, and with it Syria Palestine, was restored to Ottoman Turkish rule.

Resistance to Napoleon in Palestine had been led by Jazzar Pasha, a gifted military man and ruthless tyrant. He had been the governor of the Acre region. After the defeat of Napoleon he ruled the entire country. He now taxed the people heavily in order to rebuild and refortify Acre. To strengthen that city further, he invited merchants and financiers, notably from Damascus, Syria, to come to Acre. Through the influence of his advisor, Hayim Farhi, a Jew from Damascus, many Jews were included among the newcomers to Acre. Jazzar's adopted son, Suleiman, from 1804 to 1818 ruled as governor of the Acre district, eventually developing that city into the most important trading center of Palestine.

Suleiman died in 1818, and Hayim Farhi, who had stayed on as advisor, succeeded in placing in power a freed slave of Suleiman's named Abdallah, who promptly had Farhi beheaded and confiscated his property. Abdallah eventually was able to enlarge his rule to include the cities of Jaffa, Ramla, and Jerusalem.

The Ottoman ruler, Sultan Mahmud, appointed a general named Muhammad Ali to be governor of Egypt, with the title of "Pasha." In 1831 Pasha Muhammad Ali rebelled against the Ottoman regime, declared Egypt independent, and with his son,

Ibrahim, ruled over that land and also over the Holy Land, which at this time became known simply as Palestine. During the following period, Arab peasants rebelled against the new ruler's oppressive taxes and conscription measures. They captured Jerusalem but were in turn soon defeated.

During the ten years he ruled, Muhammad Ali introduced many modern European methods into an area that for so long had been backward. He especially admired the French, and the region began to benefit from more efficient administrative and commercial policies, largely copied from them.

France, Britain, and Russia, however, feared that Ali would make further moves to expand his power. They supported the Ottoman sultan, removed Ali and the Egyptians, and returned both Palestine and Egypt to the Ottoman rule. The Ottomans retained the more modern and effective administrative methods introduced by Ali. And they continued to open the country more and more to European influence.

Each European power that was trying to establish a foothold in this part of the East stationed its consuls and diplomatic representatives in Palestine. They also encouraged their citizens and agents to travel widely in the land. Some good roads were built. A telegraph system was set up. Eventually, in the 1880s, French interests constructed a railroad from the Mediterranean coast to Jerusalem.

Pilgrims, students, archeologists, and tourists began to visit the country. Each year thousands traveled in Palestine, some remaining there as residents. Foreign consulates and religious missions continued to expand their activities and influence. Most of them maintained their own military guards, postal services, and courts.

The Ottomans took alarm at the increasing activities of the Europeans. Wishing to keep for themselves the valuable holy places, they placed Jerusalem and southern Palestine in separate districts under the direct control of Constantinople, their capital.

Between fifteen hundred and two thousand Jews lived in Jerusalem at the beginning of the nineteenth century. By 1844 their number had increased to more than seven thousand, and they constituted over 45 percent of the city's total population. Soon afterward, Jews became the majority in Jerusalem, as they had been during the centuries when the great Temple stood on Mount Moriah. This majority continued to grow, until by 1896 Jews made up about 62 percent of the city's residents, as against about 19 percent for Christians and slightly less for Moslems. Meanwhile, the population of Jerusalem as a whole had risen rapidly— from about 15,500 in 1844 to 45,400 just fifty-two years later.

About the middle of the nineteenth century, a decisive new trend became apparent in Jewish immigration into Palestine. Previously, most Jewish settlers had been either rabbis, religious students, handworkers, or businessmen, who gravitated only to the towns, such as Jerusalem, Safed, Tiberias, and Hebron. Many of these settlers were impoverished and depended for support on contributions from Jews in other countries.

The new immigrants, on the contrary, wished to support themselves on the land as farmers, orchardists, or agricultural workers. They were mainly students and young intellectuals from European countries—especially Russia—where they had suffered discrimination and rejection, which kindled in them a burning desire to develop a homeland they could call their own.

But such immigration, though on the increase, remained scattered and slight. From time to time proposals for the extensive establishment of self-supporting Jewish colonies in Palestine would be advanced, mainly in non-Jewish government circles in Britain and France. Britain, in particular, now well entrenched in Egypt, would have welcomed a Jewish homeland in Palestine under a British "protectorate," thus strengthening its growing hold on the Middle East, as the region was now called. However, the Turkish sultan refused to grant the legal charter required for any such Jewish colony.

In the second half of the nineteenth century, an extremely wealthy banker and English Jew, Sir Moses Montefiore (1784–1885), devoted his considerable influence and resources to help the Jewish community in Palestine. He made seven trips to Palestine and was moved to sympathy by the harshness of the life there. Stirred by the growing movement of a "return to Zion," he at last, after many attempts to buy or rent land, succeeded in 1854 in purchasing from the Turkish sultan enough ground near Safed on which to settle fifty-four families. He also built an entire Jewish residential section outside the famous walls of Old Jerusalem.

Important efforts were also made by the wealthy Rothschild family of France to aid Jews who could not otherwise acquire land. Baron Edmond de Rothschild (1845–1934) invested large sums of money to buy some 125,000 acres of land. He sought thus to build up Jewish agricultural settlements and to create a wine industry in Palestine.

In 1870 an Alsatian Jew, Karl Netter, launched an agricultural school near Jaffa under the sponsorship of the Alliance Israelite Universelle of France. The school was named *Mikveh Israel* and was destined to become a training center for Jewish settlers.

They needed all the help they could get. Farming conditions were discouraging, even deplorable. There was little fertile soil to be worked. Constant battles between Bedouins and landowners had devastated the ground, and crop yields were poor. Hungry camels and goats had long ago consumed bushes and other plants needed to retain the precious moisture in arid regions. Swamps abounded. Insect pests and disease were rampant. Earthquakes, crop blights, and famines had devastated the country even further.

During the late 1870s and early 1880s a new movement made headway among Jewish students in Kharkov and other Russian cities. It called itself *BILU*, from the initial letters of the Hebrew words that meant, "House of Jacob, let us arise and go!" By 1878 the first group of BILU settlers, drawn from Jews in Russia and Rumania, had arrived and gone to work at the Mikveh Israel farm school. They included some fifteen men and one woman—all young intellectuals, but determined to become good farmers. That same year they started a pioneer settlement, *Petah Tikveh* (Gate of Hope), which failed. But in 1882 they managed to make a new start. This time Petah Tikveh survived, as the first of many similar settlements at various places in Palestine, such as *Rosh Pinah* in the Galilee, *Zichron Jacob* in Samaria, and *Rishon Le-Zion* in Judea, among others.

However scanty their knowledge of agriculture, the new pioneers were hard-working and self-sacrificing. They sought to create a wholly different way of life in their return to the soil. They were determined to make the land of Palestine fruitful once more and to give the scattered and suffering Jews of the world a sense of hope.

The pride in past and present took many forms. One of the most memorable was that of the work of Eliezar Yitzhak Perlmann (1857-1922), a Lithuanian scholar. He was passionately determined that the Hebrew language should be revived. He was the first to adopt legally a purely Hebrew name—Ben Yehuda—after his arrival in 1882. When his first son was born he kept the child apart from all who spoke anything but pure Hebrew. Ben Yehuda reassembled the language from the ancient texts and added many modern words of his own creation. Thus he became in fact the father of modern Hebrew, now spoken and written daily by millions.

By 1897 new arrivals such as these had founded the agricultural school at Mikveh Israel and eighteen farm settlements in the Galilee, Sharon, and Judah districts. The Turkish government made constant problems for these early settlers. A particular blow was Sultan Abdul-Hamid's announced decision in 1900 to enforce the law forbidding Jewish ownership of land and limiting Jewish residence in the country to three months. But this law was never strictly enforced and these early pioneers managed somehow to stay on and survive by bribing the local officials.

Adding to the dangers of early life in these agricultural settlements were the Bedouins. They indiscriminately attacked Moslem, Christian, and Jewish farms alike, often carrying off precious livestock. Coming from different countries and backgrounds, the groups of Jewish settlers had been divided, politically and otherwise, sometimes even being hostile to one another. Each colony sought to protect itself by maintaining its own guards or by trying to buy protection from neighboring Arab and Bedouin sheiks.

The raids continued, however, and the Jewish settlers found themselves forced to cooperate for self-protection. Thus unity was achieved.

The majority of Jews in the outside world paid scant attention to these developments, even though individuals or groups from time to time tried to arouse enthusiasm for the new Jewish projects in Palestine. One of the supporting groups was called "Lovers of Zion." It had originated in Odessa, Russia, and by 1890 had branches in the United States and Britain. Its purpose was "to encourage settlement in Palestine."

Between 1860 and 1890, a number of books on "Zionism" appeared in Europe, and the concept of a return to Zion took hold and grew. Both Benjamin Disraeli, British prime minister and novelist, and the British woman writer George Eliot wrote novels with Zionist themes.

"Zionism" was named for King David's hill of Zion, a symbol for Jerusalem and all Israel. It was an idea 2,500 years old—reaching back to the destruction of the first Temple and the dispersion of the Jews to Babylon and elsewhere. Yet there were still extremely religious Jews who thought a return to the homeland could only follow the appearance of a Messiah to lead them there. Zionism argued that its movement must be political and independent, that Jews must rely upon themselves to return to Israel, to cultivate its arid land and transform the country into a flourishing homeland for all Jews.

The best known among the leaders of the Zionist movement was Theodor Herzl (1860–1904), a brilliant Viennese journalist and playwright. He had almost no Jewish heritage or background. Yet, as a journalist in France, he saw the ugliness of growing anti-Semitism, which culminated finally in the notorious Dreyfus case. This involved an innocent Jewish army officer who had been crudely "framed" to cover up acts of treason by Christian fellow-officers.

Herzl came to the hard realization that there could be no end to the growing persecutions of Jews so long as they remained helpless "outsiders" in nations that at best tolerated them. He concluded that only if Jews created a state of their own, a homeland, could they live in dignity and safety. He dedicated his talents, his money, and his life to the effort to found somehow, somewhere, such a Jewish state. Time and again Herzl sought the aid of leading statesmen of Europe to help in persuading the sultan in Constantinople to grant the charter or permission that would make possible Jewish colonization in Palestine, always his first choice for that essential Jewish homeland.

The story of Herzl's appeals to the sultan, to the kaiser of Germany, to the pope in Rome, and to financiers and ministers of government is a long, heartbreaking one. It indeed amounts to an epic and a private tragedy at the same time, though in the larger and later sense, as seen from the vantage point of the 1970s, it has been crowned by a triumph unique in the world's history: the reemergence of a firm and functioning Jewish homeland amid the predatory nations of the modern world and on the very site of the "promised land" of the ancient Israelites.

Herzl, because of his utterly "assimilated" background, was not at first aware of the prior and current work that others had done and were doing along the lines he favored. Yet he concluded, by his own unaided analysis, that the only real hope lay in organizing the Jewish people themselves for action in their own interest and defense: They could no longer wait for an outside power or person to do their work for them.

In 1896 appeared Herzl's historic book, *The Jewish State*, proclaiming his ideas to the world. Late in August of 1897 the first World Zionist Congress assembled at Basle, Switzerland, in response to his summons. It was attended by 197 representative Jews from all over Europe, Africa, and America. A series of such congresses followed. Ultimately the Zionist Congress had two goals: the establishment of modern cooperative Jewish settlements in Palestine, and the encouragement of practical political activity by Jews in the rest of the world.

At this first World Congress the emblem that has become the flag of the modern nation of Israel was proposed and adopted.

Its blue star was the famous "Star of David." Its blue stripes on a white background are reminiscent of the Jewish prayer shawls or *tallesim*.

The Congress met both with hostility and with some enthusiasm from Jews and gentiles of the world.

In 1901 the Jewish National Fund was set up to purchase land for Jewish use in Palestine. Zionists over the world levied on themselves a yearly membership payment (called the *shekel*) and also solicited contributions to help the Fund. In spite of inadequate finances and the outlandishly increased prices set by Arab and Turkish landowners, the Fund continued to acquire land. Jewish colonies, agricultural ventures, and schools continued gradually to grow in numbers, even though the basic idea of the establishment of a Jewish state was blocked by the Turkish government.

Finally, after countless disappointments, the British government, through its colonial secretary, Joseph Chamberlain, offered to the Jews Uganda in British East Africa to use as a colony. Desperate, Herzl presented the proposal to the Sixth Zionist Congress in 1903. But the idea of a return to Palestine as their proper homeland was too strong in the minds of the delegates. They rejected the British offer at their Seventh Congress in 1905.

Herzl had already died in 1904 at the age of forty-four. His remains today have a place of honor on a hillside in Jerusalem, capital of the new state of Israel.

Further shocking pogroms in Russia and Poland in 1907 and 1908 brought a large influx of Jews to Israel. Among these arrivals were those who were instrumental in founding the defense group called *Bar Giora*, which later became the *Ha Shomer*. They worked both as guards and as farmers, and stressed united defense for all the Jews of the land. They rejected the idea of hiring Arab guards, believing that Jews should protect Jews, and that the "honor" of Jews, as well as their lives and property, should be preserved. In the beginning there were only ten such dedicated guards. Between them they had but one rifle, one pistol, and one dagger. To make up for lack of equipment, they purposely dressed in flashy uniforms to impress the Arabs.

By 1910 they were able to add horses and boots to their equipment. Their number soon grew to 150, guarding twenty agricultural settlements. It was not long before the Ha Shomer guard in his braid-trimmed uniform with cartridge belt and sword became legend throughout Europe's Jewish communities. Countless young people yearned to reach Israel, where a Jew did not have to bow before the yoke of oppression but could hold up his head proudly, and even ride horses and carry arms.

Before World War I (1914–1918), the Jewish population of Palestine had risen to 100,000, out of a total population of 700,000. In Jerusalem by 1910, of about 74,000 inhabitants, 47,400 were Jewish. Secular schools, libraries, art schools, and some industry sprang up, adding to the already established Jewish religious institutions of the city. There was even a strike in the printing trades in Jerusalem in 1907, led by Izhak Ben Zvi, a labor Zionist, later to become president of Israel.

A new breed of Jews was arising—hard-working, sturdy, healthy, and unafraid—able to protect, hold, and develop the land of Israel.

15

"NEXT YEAR IN JERUSALEM"

(TO 1948, YEAR OF THE DECLARATION
OF INDEPENDENCE OF ISRAEL)

"Next year in Jerusalem!"

> —Traditional exclamation uttered, during centuries
> past, twice each year: at the Passover meal
> (Seder), and on the Day of Atonement (Yom
> Kippur) after the blowing of the ram's horn
> (Shofar) at the close of the Neilah service.

During World War I (1914–1918), Turkey sided with Germany and Austria against the Allies (Britain, France, Italy, and finally the United States). It brought a bad time for the Jews in Palestine and halted further Jewish settlement there. The enemies of Turkey now included Britain, which since 1882 had been entrenched in Egypt, and which for some time had looked with favor on furthering large-scale Jewish colonization in Palestine. The Turks tried early in the war to win control of the Suez Canal area between Palestine and Egypt, but they were driven off.

In Palestine under Turkish rule, Jews suspected of sympathizing with Britain were hanged, and Zionism was outlawed. Twelve thousand Jews were deported from the country on the pretext that they did not have Turkish citizenship. The population of Palestine decreased.

This dismal situation was finally relieved by a series of distant events. Chaim Weizmann, a British scientist and dedicated Zionist, later to become the first president of the state of Israel, had been largely instrumental in developing the explosive called TNT, so important to Great Britain in the war. Thus he was able to gain sympathetic audience with members of the British government and in particular with the foreign secretary, Arthur James Balfour. Weizmann proposed that Britain plan to set up a protectorate in Palestine and to establish there a national home for the Jews.

One of the motives for Britain's affirmative decision was no doubt a desire to secure a stronger hold in the Middle East. That decision took the form of the Balfour Declaration of November 2, 1917, and paved the way for the Jewish state. The Declaration avowed that Great Britain would do its best to establish such a home for Jews in Palestine, provided that the religious and civil rights of the non-Jewish population of the country, or the rights of Jews in other countries, not be impaired.

In the meantime, in June of 1917, General Sir Edmund Allenby was appointed commander of British forces in the Middle East. He intensified the attack against the Turkish army in Palestine and Syria. While the Turks and their German allies were strengthening the defenses around Jerusalem, Allenby captured Beersheba on October 21, 1917. He then moved his forces northward through the desert to a position west of Jerusalem. Here on December 8 and 9 a fierce battle took place. It ended in victory for the British.

On December 9, General Allenby led his men to Jerusalem itself. It was the first day of Hanukkah, the holiday which in the Jewish calendar commemorates the victory in 164 B.C.E. of the Maccabean forces over the Seleucid regime.

General Allenby dismounted from his horse and entered the sacred city on foot. No blood was shed as Great Britain's soldiers occupied the sites that had seen so many other conquerors come and go during past millennia.

By September of 1918 the British fighting men had occupied also the remainder of Palestine.

In these conquests, the British allowed the Jews to have little or no part. A Jewish Legion was authorized and the recruitment of volunteers to fill its ranks was begun early in 1918. But three battalions, once formed, were kept stalled in Egypt. In November 1918, the First World War ended with the victory of the Allies and the signing of the Armistice. After that the Jewish Legion was assigned to service in distant and desolate Sinai.

Though robbed of a role in liberating their land from Turkish rule, many Jewish Legionnaires gained important experience for their future. The ranks of the organizers of the Legion included Joseph Trumpeldor, the fabulous one-armed Jewish military hero, once an officer of the Tsar's army in Russia. Another organizer was Zev (Vladimir) Jabotinsky, an outstanding Jewish militant and intellectual.

On April 25, 1920, the Allied powers appointed Great Britain the "mandatory" or governing power for Palestine as well as Mesopotamia (later renamed Iraq) and other countries. The terms of this mandate were approved by the newly formed League of Nations (to which the United States never belonged).

In 1920, a month after the mandate became effective, Sir Herbert Samuel, a British Jew high in government circles, was appointed the first high commissioner for Palestine. Under the mandate, Great Britain administered the country of Palestine, and with the way open for colonization, Jewish immigration to Palestine increased again.

There were scarcely 35,000 Jews in all the country at the time. But huge numbers of Jews now flocked to Palestine—mainly from eastern Europe. Jewish intellectual life made great strides, and the country developed economically. On Mount Scopus overlooking Jerusalem, a medical center, a national library, and the Hebrew University were founded.

One of the Jews who returned after the British conquest of Palestine was David Ben Gurion, later to become the state of Israel's first prime minister as well as its first minister of defense. Born in Poland in 1886, he had first reached Palestine as a settler when only twenty years old. His persistent political activity on behalf of his fellow Jews so enraged the Turkish government that he was arrested and sentenced to death. The sentence, however, was commuted, and in 1914 he was deported along with Izhak Ben Zvi, who became the second president of Israel. For a time Ben Gurion lived in the United States, but he returned later to serve as a corporal in the British army in the campaign to take Palestine.

In Palestine after World War I, Ben Gurion was instrumental in building the *Haganah,* the secret or unofficial defense force of Palestine's Jews, which eventually developed into the powerfully effective army of Israel.

As Jewish life expanded, Arab nationalism grew. Resentment

flared against Zionism, against the British Mandate, and against the influx of Jews into the country. Blood was shed as disorders led by Arab political and religious leaders erupted, notably in a three-day riot in Jerusalem in 1920 in which a number of Jews were killed. In the same year, the community of Tel Hai was attacked. Here the Israeli hero Joseph Trumpeldor was killed. There were further Arab riots in Jaffa in 1921.

In an attempt to placate the Arab population, Britain, in June of 1922, issued the so-called Churchill White Paper, limiting Jewish immigration and land purchases in Palestine. Further, it removed the region called Trans-Jordan from the mandated territories which were to provide a "National Home for the Jews." That withdrawn area was given an Arab government and ultimately became known as the "Hashemite Kingdom of Transjordan." Jews, in fact, were forbidden to settle there. Jordan, known in biblical days as the lands of Edom and Moab, was given its independence by Great Britain in 1936.

Opposition to the Churchill White Paper was voiced by Zev Jabotinsky and others. In 1925 Jabotinsky founded the Revisionist Party, which was highly militant in its Zionist aims. He and his followers were drastically opposed to the limitations in this White Paper. They denounced Dr. Chaim Weizmann's policy of cooperation with Great Britain in this respect and demanded immediate and complete fulfillment by Britain's Palestine government of the promised National Home for the Jews. They looked upon non-Zionist Jews as traitors.

By late 1925 there were some one hundred Jewish settlements throughout Palestine, with a combined population of about 83,-000. Six years later, the country's Jewish population had risen to 175,000, of whom about 51,000 lived in Jerusalem, where they comprised more than 60 percent of the residents.

In 1929 a riot erupted, triggered by Arab irritation at the blowing of the ram's horn (*Shofar*) at the Western ("Wailing") Wall on the Day of Atonement (*Yom Kippur*). The disturbances quickly spread throughout the country, with a loss of 133 Jews killed, several hundred wounded, and much Jewish property damaged. The Jewish community of Hebron was totally destroyed, and Safed was hard hit. These attacks served to initiate a new era and new Jewish attitudes toward self-defense. The Haganah had been organized in the first place essentially to protect agricultural settlements and towns against Arab guerrilla raids. Now it was strengthened in both men and materials, and some leaders began to insist that a still more active defense organization was urgently needed.

In the meantime, as the Jewish population increased, so did development of the country. Old cities were expanded and modernized, and new ones arose. Rural settlements were located all the way from the Syrian border in the north to the edges of the Negev desert in the south and even beyond. With their energy and intelligence the new agriculturists reclaimed swamps, sand dunes, and infertile areas. They treated the soil with all the means of modern science. Water was brought in, citrus groves were developed, wheat was grown. To this day, Israel is noted for its agricultural collectives (*kibbutzim*) and cooperatives (*moshavim*)—both being communes where the products of joint labor are shared.

The advent to power of Adolf Hitler in Germany in 1933 brought additional Jewish refugees to the shores of Palestine, increasing its Jewish population to more than 400,000—still a minority in the country, however. In 1935 alone, 62,000 victims of Nazi oppression landed in the Holy Land. These earlier German Jews, who managed to escape before the full force of the Nazi crackdown, brought to Palestine money, economic resources, skill, and knowledge which greatly benefited the development of the country. Many settled in the Sharon district along the coast; others joined Jewish settlements elsewhere in Palestine and strengthened Jewish communities in spite of continual Arab threats and attacks. But many did not reach the shores of Palestine. Under Adolf Hitler, millions were victims of the Nazi concentration camps and gas ovens.

Almost continual violent Arab anti-Jewish riots between 1936 and 1939 threatened the lives of the Jewish residents of the cities and the settlers on the land. When the 1936 riots led to an Arab general strike, which cut off food supplies, the Jews soon learned how to survive—an enormous advantage in later conflicts with the Arabs.

Long before that, the Jews of Palestine had reached the conclusion that they must strengthen their military defenses. Their cities as well as their agricultural settlements needed protection. Under the Mandate, there had evolved from the original armed guards (Ha Shomer) of the early period of settlement the underground Haganah defense force. In 1939 the Haganah developed a spectacular fighting force called the *Palmach*.

Much valuable training in methods still used by the Israeli army today was given by a sympathetic British captain, Orde Wingate. Beginning in 1937, and for a year and a half before he was ousted from the country by the British, he instructed the embryo army in most unorthodox but extremely effective military methods. Additional military experience was later acquired by Palestinian Jews who fought in the British army against the Germans in World War II.

In 1939 there were approximately half a million Jews in Palestine and about twice as many Arabs. The British had brought a relatively efficient and orderly administration to the land. They were interested in keeping the peace, but even more interested in keeping intact the flow of petroleum from the Arab countries that possessed this "black gold." Hence the British government went along with the demands of anti-Zionist Arab leaders, even when these violated the pledges of its mandate over Palestine.

In this same year, under Prime Minister Neville Chamberlain, the British government issued another White Paper, further reducing and virtually ending Jewish immigration into Palestine. Under the terms of this Paper, only seventy-five thousand immigrants were to be allowed to enter during the next five years; Arab consent would have to be obtained for any number beyond this. Also, severe restrictions were placed on the amount of land that Jews could purchase from Arabs. At its expiration the British mandate was to be replaced by an independent government in which Arabs would be in the majority.

In effect, this 1939 White Paper threatened the existence of the Jews already in Palestine and placed them at the mercy of the

Arabs. Also it would lock the gates against Jews who were desperately seeking to flee from the Hitler persecution in Germany, Austria, and Czechoslovakia.

Bitter and widespread Jewish protest followed, not only in Palestine but elsewhere in the world where the cause of Zionism was supported. When Hitler's attack on Poland in the autumn of 1939 set off World War II, the situation altered sharply. Now there seemed to be no way, short of the defeat of Hitler, to rescue the Jews still under Nazi power in Germany, Austria, and the other countries that his armies quickly conquered. The cause of Great Britain, principal opponent of Hitler Germany, necessarily became also the cause of the Jews of Palestine. They declared that the war against Hitler Germany was their war.

During World War II, accordingly, many Palestinian Jews served with the British forces against the Germans and their Italian allies. They fought during the five and a half long, bitter and bloody years of the most colossal war in the history of mankind. Stupendous losses took place in property and human lives—not only among combatants, but also, during the last years of the war, among millions of civilian Jews who were rounded up from all areas controlled by the German Nazis and slaughtered.

In extermination centers all over Europe built for this purpose, between five and six million Jews of all ages, as well as a huge number of non-Jews of many ethnic backgrounds, were gassed, shot, burned, and otherwise destroyed. Nothing like it had ever happened before.

By the end of the war, with Hitler dead and Germany defeated, vast numbers of Jewish refugees who had somehow survived the mass destruction were desperate to find safe homes. Many nations, including the United States, closed their doors against these brutally treated Nazi victims. The Jews of Palestine desperately wanted and tried to bring these refugees into the land that had been intended as a "homeland" for all Jews.

Nevertheless, after the end of the war in 1945, the new Labor government in Britain sought to impose the same harsh terms as the objectionable White Paper that Chamberlain had unveiled in 1939. Petroleum was still a power in the world.

Then Zionists, inside and outside Palestine, pointed constantly to the obligation of the British government: Great Britain's presence and control over Palestine was dependent on the establishment there of a national home for the Jews.

When the anti-immigration policies of the British authorities continued even in the face of the urgent plight of homeless refugees, the Palestinian Jews intensified a program of active "noncooperation." With the help of world Jewry, they acquired ships to transport Jewish refugees from Europe to Israel. A coastal blockade was established by the British to prevent these "illegals" from being landed, and a number of such ships were halted.

Most of the captured vessels were taken to the island of Cyprus, where the Jews were once again penned up in camps. One vessel, the *Exodus*, was even forced to return all the way to Europe with its load of embittered and desperate refugees.

Despite all the dangers and the threats, thousands succeeded in getting through illegally, however, and became residents of Israel.

Increasingly, Jewish leaders reached the unwelcome conclusion that Great Britain would no longer respond to either diplomatic representations or peaceful protests. Heads of the official Zionist organization in Palestine came finally to much the same view that many years earlier had been urged so emphatically by Zev Jabotinsky when he founded the illegal activist force called the *Irgun*.

Seeing no hope of persuading the Labor government of Britain to abandon its White Paper policies, Jewish leaders in Palestine became more militant. In a similar way, during the first century C.E., the Pharisees were forced to give up pacifism and to accept the Zealots' demands for open resistance to Rome. Increasingly the Haganah, instead of actively restraining or passively opposing the Irgun's projects, tolerated and sometimes even helped them. British buildings and personnel in Palestine came under attack by Jewish militant groups in spectacular actions designed both to alert the world to the intolerable situation of the Jews and to force the British to change their anti-Zionist policies. Such actions were undertaken by groups of the Irgun, by the so-called Stern Gang, and even at times by elements of the Palmach, the fighting commando group of the Haganah itself.

Two tormented and dramatic years, beginning in the latter part of 1945, were punctuated by bold, incredible acts of protest and resistance. These included even the freeing of Jewish prisoners from well-guarded British jails, the sinking of British naval vessels offshore, and the destruction of railway lines and oil refineries. When questioned by British authorities, leaders denied any knowledge of the plans, preparations, and personnel behind these spectacular acts of defiance and protest.

By the middle of 1947 it had become clear to almost all competent outside observers that Palestine could be freed from violence and bloodshed only if some rational way were found to separate and satisfy the demands of the Jewish residents on the one hand and the Arabs on the other.

It was the newly formed United Nations, dedicated to the hope of avoiding further warfare and destruction in the world, that worked out an important proposal and laid it before all parties. That young organization, which this time included the United States as well as Britain and other major powers, voted on November 29, 1947, that Palestine should be partitioned into two separate but contiguous countries, Jewish and Arab. Jerusalem, sacred to both groups, was to become an "international enclave" or zone available to all.

The Jews of Palestine were overjoyed.

The very next day, however, Arab nationalists launched a series of bombing attacks, killing dozens of Jews and destroying many structures in the modern Jewish section of Jerusalem, often called "the New City." With help from some individuals in the British Mandate government, the Arabs were able to block the supply road to Jerusalem and to destroy that city's water pipeline. Within Jerusalem, they occupied the Hadassah Hospital and the Hebrew University on Mount Scopus to the north, and took control of the Jewish quarter near the Western Wall in the Old City.

Arab attacks continued on settlements and villages throughout the rest of Palestine, with the Jewish population grimly resisting, determined to hold on to the cherished land. Jewish convoys carrying food and arms to outlying settlements were repeatedly attacked by Arabs. War again had come to Israel.

The historic town of Safed in the Galilee was cut off and be-

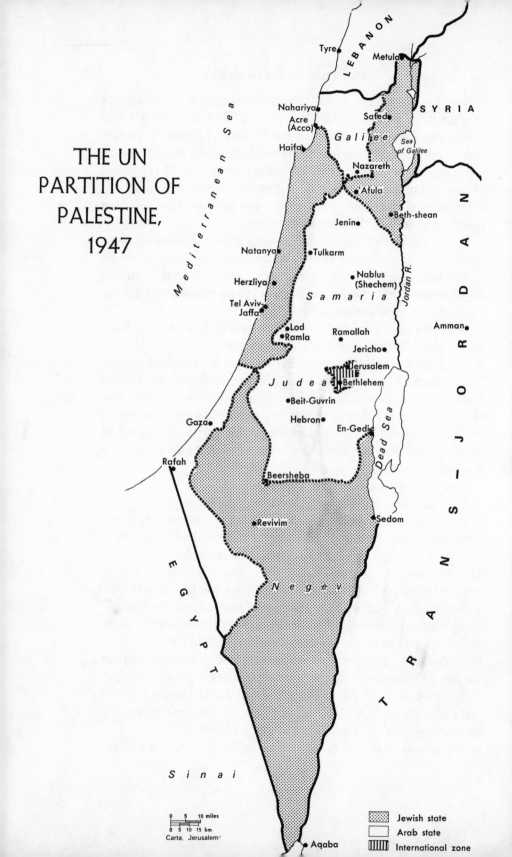

THE UN
PARTITION OF
PALESTINE,
1947

Mediterranean Sea

LEBANON

Tyre

Metula

S Y R I A

Nahariya

Safed

Acre
(Acco)

Galilee

Haifa

*Sea
of Galilee*

Nazareth

Afula

Beth-shean

Jenin

Natanya

Tulkarm

Herzliya

Nablus
(Shechem)

S a m a r i a

Jordan R.

Tel Aviv-
Jaffa

Lod

Ramla

Ramallah

Amman

Jericho

Jerusalem

J u d e a

Bethlehem

Beit-Guvrin

Gaza

Hebron

En-Gedi

Dead Sea

Rafah

Beersheba

Revivim

Sedom

N e g e v

T R A N S - J O R D A N

E G Y P T

S i n a i

| 0 | 5 | 10 miles |
| 0 | 5 | 10 | 15 km |

Carta, Jerusalem

Aqaba

▓ Jewish state

☐ Arab state

▥ International zone

sieged by the Arabs for some six months. Here religious Jews dug trenches and worked on building defenses even on the Sabbath. The story is told of one of the rabbis, Abraham Zira, who put on his best holiday clothes and, followed by his disciples, went out to do the holy work of defending the town. Safed's eventual rescue and liberation is an exciting story.

In the new part of the city of Jerusalem, the besieged Jews were sustained by their high morale and determination. They were able to hold on until convoys of food and supplies finally could force their way through to them.

Battles continued throughout Palestine. The Jewish Haganah and Palmach forces, though inferior to the Arabs in numbers and equipment, fought with unusual bravery and determination. The rusted wrecks of Haganah armored vehicles from those struggles of 1947 and 1948 can still be seen beside the road to Jerusalem—a grim reminder of the troubled days before statehood.

In the midst of this undeclared war, which had now lasted some five and a half months, on May 15, 1948 the British Mandate officially expired. The Jews of Palestine announced to the world that they had formed a new, independent state. They chose for it what seemed an inevitable name—Israel! It was to become in fact as well as intent the land of the Jews, of all Jews seeking to share its mingled security and dangers.

The following text* of the historic Proclamation of Independence, dated Friday, May 14, 1948, reviews the past, the purposes, and the hopes of the new state.

The Land of Israel was the birthplace of the Jewish people. Here their spiritual, religious, and national identity was formed. Here they achieved independence and created a culture of national and universal significance. Here they wrote and gave the Bible to the world.

Exiled from the Land of Israel, the Jewish people remained

---

* Brief omissions in the text are indicated by ellipses (...).

faithful to it in all the countries of their dispersion, never ceasing
to pray and hope for their return and the restoration of their
national freedom.

. . . Jews strove throughout the centuries to go back to the
land of their fathers and regain their statehood. In recent decades
they returned in their masses. They reclaimed the wilderness,
revived their language, built cities and villages, and established a
vigorous and ever-growing community, with its own economic
and cultural life. They sought peace, yet were prepared to defend
themselves. They brought the blessings of progress to all inhabitants of the country and looked forward to sovereign independence.

In the year 1897, the first Zionist Congress, inspired by Theodor Herzl's vision of the Jewish State, proclaimed the right
of the Jewish people to national revival in their own country.

This right was acknowledged by the Balfour Declaration of
November 2, 1917, and re-affirmed by the Mandate of the League
of Nations, which gave explicit international recognition to the
historic connection of the Jewish people with Palestine and their
right to reconstitute their National Home.

The recent holocausts, which engulfed millions of Jews in
Europe, proved anew the need to solve the problem of the home-
lessness and lack of independence of the Jewish people by means
of the re-establishment of the Jewish State, which would open
the gates to all Jews and endow the Jewish people with equality
of status among the family of nations.

The survivors of the disastrous slaughter in Europe, and also
Jews from other lands, have not desisted from their efforts to
reach *Eretz-Yisrael*, in the face of difficulties, obstacles and perils;
and have not ceased to urge their right to a life of dignity, freedom, and honest toil in their ancestral land.

In the Second World War, the Jewish people in Palestine
made their full contribution to the struggle of the freedom-loving
nations against the Nazi evil. The sacrifices of their soldiers and
their war effort gained them the right to rank with the nations
which founded the United Nations.

On November 29, 1947, The General Assembly of the United

Nations adopted a Resolution requiring the establishment of a Jewish State in Palestine. The General Assembly [of the UN] called upon the inhabitants of the country to take all the necessary steps on their part to put the plan into effect. This recognition by the UN of the right of the Jewish people to establish their independent State is unassailable.

It is the natural right of the Jewish people to lead—as so all other nations—an independent existence in its sovereign State.

ACCORDINGLY, WE, the members of the National Council, representing the Jewish people in Palestine and the World Zionist Movement, are met together in solemn assembly today, the day of the termination of the British Mandate for Palestine; and by virtue of the natural and historic right of the Jewish people and of the Resolution of the General Assembly of the UN,

WE HEREBY PROCLAIM the establishment of the Jewish State in Palestine, to be called *Medinath Yisrael* (The State of Israel).

WE HEREBY DECLARE that . . . pending the setting up of the duly-elected bodies of the State in accordance with a Constitution, to be drawn up . . . not later than the 1st of October, 1948, the National Council shall act as the Provisional State Council, and that the National Administration shall constitute the Provisional Government of the Jewish state. . . .

THE STATE OF ISRAEL will be open to the immigration of Jews from all the countries of their dispersion; it will promote the development of the country for the benefit of all its inhabitants; will be based on the principles of liberty, justice, and peace as conceived by the Prophets of Israel; will uphold the full social and political equality of all its citizens, without distinction of religion, race, or sex; will guarantee freedom of religion, conscience, education and culture; will safeguard the Holy Places of all religions; and will loyally uphold the principles of the UN Charter.

We appeal to the UN to assist the Jewish people in the building of its State and to admit Israel into the family of nations.

In the midst of wanton aggression, we yet call upon the Arab inhabitants of the State of Israel to preserve the ways of peace and play their part in the development of the State, on the basis of full and equal citizenship and due representation in all its bodies and institutions—provisional and permanent.

We extend our hand in peace and neighborliness to all the neighboring states and their peoples, and invite them to cooperate with the independent Jewish nation for the common good of all. The State of Israel is prepared to make its contribution to the progress of the Middle East as a whole.

Our call goes out to the Jewish people all over the world to rally to our side in the task of immigration and development, and to stand by in the great struggle for the fulfillment of the dream of generations for the redemption of Israel.

. . . we set our hand to this Declaration . . . on this Sabbath eve, the fifth of *Iyar*, 5708, the fourteenth of May, 1948.

This proclamation, like previous assertions of the rights and aims of the Jews in their historic land, served only as a prelude to further trials. The warfare continued. Arab units clashed with the Jewish forces. Bitter battles were followed by occasional cease-fires or truces, as efforts were made to find a basis for halting the bloodshed.

Both sides desperately sought to retain all of Jerusalem. Neither was wholly successful. Armistice agreements worked out between February and April of 1949 left Jerusalem itself divided. Jordan, the Arab nation to the east, held the Old City, the onetime Temple site on Mount Moriah, as well as the Mount of Olives, Mount Scopus, and many other historic areas. Included was the famous Western Wall, the last surviving remnant of the great Temple destroyed by the Romans in the first century C.E. On the platform above that Western (or "Wailing") Wall stands the present Haram containing the Dome of the Rock, and the el Aksa Mosque, both sacred to Islam because their site is associated with prophets revered in their religion—David, Solomon, and Mohammed himself.

ISRAEL AFTER THE SIX-DAY WAR

CEASE-FIRE LINES OF JUNE 1967

(COMPARED WITH ARMISTICE LINES OF 1949)

Mediterranean Sea

Beirut

Sidon

Damascus

LEBANON

Tyre

Kuneitra

SYRIA

Acre (Acco)

Safed

Sea of Galilee

Haifa

Galilee

Nazareth

Der'aa

Jenin

Natanya

Samaria

Nablus

Jordan R.

Petah Tikva

Tel Aviv-Jaffa

Salt

Ramla

Ramallah

Amman

Modi'in

Jericho

Ashdod

Jerusalem

Judea

Gaza

Hebron

Dead Sea

Masada

Kerak

Beersheba

JORDAN

Dimona

Negev

Port-Sa'id

El-Arish

Kantara

Kusseima

Mizpe-Ramon

Ismailia

Bir Gafgafa

Ma'an

Suez

Kal'at en-Nakhel

Kuntilla

EGYPT

Ras-Suder

Eilat

Aqaba

Sinai

Gulf of Suez

Gulf of Eilat

Nuweiba

SAUDI

Ras Abu Rudeis

ARABIA

▲Mt. Sinai

Dahab

Et-Tur

Tiran

Sharm e-Sheikh

Sanafir

▪▪▪▪▪ Armistice lines, 1949

⋮⋮⋮ Administered by Israel

Red Sea

0   20   40 miles

0 20 40 60 km

Carta, Jerusalem

The new state of Israel retained the newer, western parts of Jerusalem. Between the two parts of the city ran a ragged, jagged, ugly no-man's-land marked by barbed wire and armed patrols. Jordanian authorities refused to admit Jews from Israel to visit the site of the former Temple, or even—despite the terms of the truce—to pray at the Western Wall below it.

Once again, as so often during the more than nineteen hundred years preceding, Jews were barred from peaceful visits to the site of the former Temples and from their traditional place of lamentation and worship, the symbolic Wall.

Eighteen years later, after the Six-Day War of June 1967, the Israelis, as they are now called, were able at last to return.

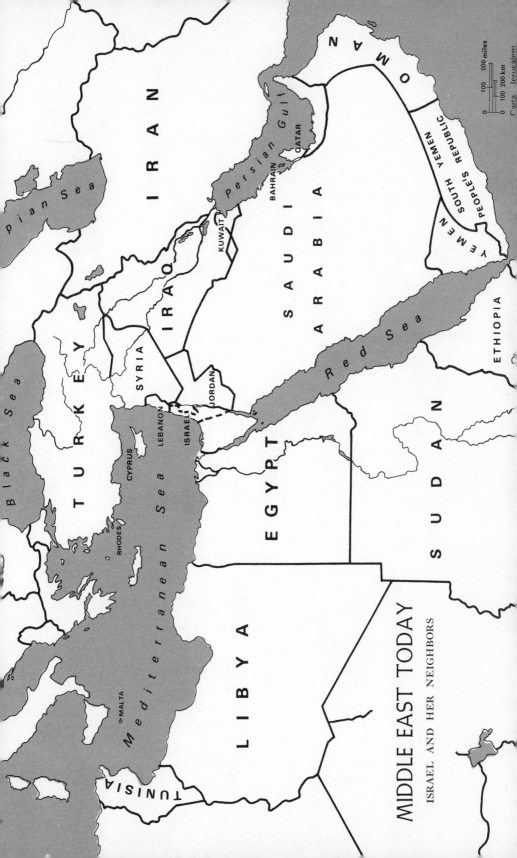

MIDDLE EAST TODAY

ISRAEL AND HER NEIGHBORS

BIBLIOGRAPHY

AHARONI, YOHANON, *The Land of the Bible* (Philadelphia, 1967)

AHARONI, YOHANON, and AVI-YONAH, MICHAEL, *The Macmillan Bible Atlas* (N.Y., 1968)

AVI-YONAH, MICHAEL, *A History of the Holy Land* (London, 1969)

AVI-YONAH, MICHAEL, *The Holy Land from the Persian to the Arab Conquest—A Historical Geography* (Grand Rapids, 1966)

AVI-YONAH, MICHAEL (editor), *Jerusalem* (N.Y., 1960)

BEN GURION, DAVID (editor), *The Jews in Their Land* (Garden City, N.Y., 1966)

BENTWICH, NORMAN, *Israel Resurgent* (N.Y., 1960)

BORSCHENIUS, PAUL, *The History of the Jews* (N.Y., 1965). 5 volumes. Translated from the Danish

BOUDET, J. (editor), *Jerusalem, A History* (N.Y., 1967)

BRIGHT, JOHN, *A History of Israel* (Philadelphia, 1959)

CORNILL, C. H., *History of the People of Israel* (La Salle, Ill., 1943). First published in 1898

DIMONT, MAX I., *Jews, God, and History* (N.Y., 1962)

DUBNOV, SIMON, *History of the Jews* (N.Y., 1968). 2 volumes

EBAN, ABBA, *My People—The Story of the Jews* (N.Y., 1968)

EHRLICH, ERNST LUDWIG, *A Concise History of Israel* (N.Y., 1962). Translated from the German

ELON, AMOS, *The Israelis* (N.Y., 1971)

EPSTEIN, ISIDORE, *Judaism, A Historical Presentation* (Baltimore, 1960)

FINKELSTEIN, LOUIS (editor), *The Jews—Their History, Culture, and Religion.* 2 volumes (N.Y., 1949)

GOLDMANN, EVA and ZEEV, and WIMMER, HED, *A Land That I Will Show Thee—The Jewish People Through the Ages* (N.Y., 1968)

BIBLIOGRAPHY

GRAETZ, HEINRICH, *History of the Jews* (Philadelphia, 1891-8). 6 volumes

KIRK, G. E., *A Short History of the Middle East* (N.Y., 1959)

KLEIN, MINA C. and H. ARTHUR, *Temple Beyond Time—The Story of the Site of Solomon's Temple* (N.Y., 1970)

KRAELING, EMIL G., *Bible Atlas* (N.Y., 1956)

LARTÉGUY, JEAN, *The Walls of Israel* (N.Y., 1969). Translated from the French

LE STRANGE, GUY, *Palestine Under the Moslems* (Beirut, Lebanon, 1965). A reissue of the original 1890 edition

LEARSI, RUFUS (GOLDBERG, ISRAEL), *A History of the Jewish People* (Cleveland, 1949)

MARGOLIS, MAX LEOPOLD, and MARX, ALEXANDER, *A History of the Jewish People* (Philadelphia, 1927)

PARKES, JAMES, *A History of the Jewish People* (Baltimore, 1964). A Penguin paperback

PARKES, JAMES, *Whose Land? A History of the Peoples of Palestine* (Baltimore, 1970). A Penguin paperback

RADDOCK, CHARLES, *Portrait of a People* (N.Y., 1967). 3 volumes

RATTEY, B. K., *A Short History of the Hebrews* (London, 1964). Written 1931

ROTH, CECIL, *History of the Jews* (N.Y., 1961)

RUNCIMAN, STEVEN, *A History of the Crusades* (N.Y., 1951). 3 volumes

SACHAR, A. L., *A History of the Jews* (N.Y., 5th edition, 1965)

SCHÜRER, EMIL, *A History of the Jewish People in the Time of Jesus* (N. Y., 1961). An abridgment of the first English edition of 1886-90

TCHERIKOVER, V., *Hellenistic Civilization and the Jews* (Philadelphia, 1961)

TELLER, JUDD, *Biography of a People* (N.Y., 1966)

WOLLMAN-TSAMIR, PINCHAS (editor), *Graphic History of the Jewish Heritage* (N.Y., 1963)

INDEX

ABOUT THE AUTHORS

MINA C. KLEIN, born near London, lived first in Canada, then in California. She attended school in Los Angeles, Berlin, and New York City.

H. ARTHUR KLEIN, Manhattan born, came to California as a boy. He was graduated from Stanford University and received a master's degree from Occidental College. He has taught English and German at the college level.

After meeting in Los Angeles, the Kleins married in Berlin, where Mr. Klein worked as feature writer for American news services. The Kleins are widely traveled and have more than once visited Israel. Besides travel, their principal recreations are reading, walking, and listening to recorded music.

They now live and write in their home beside the Pacific, in Malibu, California. They have a daughter and a son. Writing together and separately they have been responsible for some fourteen books. Among the books they have written together are:

KÄTHE KOLLWITZ: Life in Art
TEMPLE BEYOND TIME—The Story of the Site of Solomon's Temple
PETER BRUEGEL THE ELDER, ARTIST OF ABUNDANCE
GREAT STRUCTURES OF THE WORLD
SURF'S UP! An Anthology of Surfing